Making Sense, Shaping Meaning

Writing in the Context of a Capacity-Based Approach to Learning

Pat D'Arcy

BOYNTON/COOK PUBLISHERS
HEINEMANN
PORTSMOUTH, NH

BOYNTON/COOK PUBLISHERS, INC.
A Subsidiary of
HEINEMANN EDUCATIONAL BOOKS, INC.
361 Hanover Street   Portsmouth, NH   03801-3959
Offices and agents throughout the world

The following have generously given permission to use quotations from copyrighted works:

Page 43: From *Write to Learn* by Donald M. Murray. Published by Holt, Rinehart & Winston, 1984, 1987. Used by permission.

Page 84: "Winter" by Judith Nicholls. Reprinted by permission of Faber and Faber Ltd from *The Midnight Forest* by Judith Nichols.

Page 119: From "Writing to Learn" by Pat D'Arcy in *The Journal Book*, edited by Toby Fulwiler. Copyright © 1987 by Boynton/Cook Publishers, Inc.

Page 124: "The Arrival of the Bee Box" by Sylvia Plath, copyright © 1963 by the Estate of Sylvia Plath. Taken from *The Collected Poems of Sylvia Plath*. Reprinted by permission of Harper & Row, Publishers, Inc.

Library of Congress Cataloging-in-Publication Data
D'Arcy, Pat.
      Making sense, shaping meaning : writing in the context of a
capacity-based approach to learning / Pat D'Arcy.
          p.   cm.
      Bibliography: p.
      ISBN 0-86709-245-9
      1. Creative writing (Elementary education)   2. Learning,
Psychology of.   I. Title.
LB1576.D237   1989
372.6'23—dc20   89-31481
                                                                          CIP

Designed by Vic Schwarz.
Printed in the United States of America.
91 92 93 9 8 7 6 5 4 3 2

In memory of Mike Binks and Robin Tanner—

*both passionate believers
in the meaning-shaping
powers of all children.*

Contents

Preface

This book is really about "learning"—about how any of us, age five or fifty, make sense of our lives in the process of day-to-day living in school, at home, at work. Wherever we happen to be, in rural, small town or inner city environments, this need to make sense and shape meaning is a powerful one; what's more it doesn't cease to be a need once the demands of compulsory schooling are left behind. Far from it!

Whether we find ourselves still directly linked to our country's education system as a teacher or indirectly as a parent or a school governor (or blessedly free of any school connections whatsoever . . .) all of us continue to recollect past experiences, to reconstruct according to the demands of the present and to share our current perceptions in our homes, in pubs, at parties and so on, as well as more formally through books, articles, radio and television.

The "fat" chapters of the book focus on writing as one powerful mode of expression among many. That is because I happen to have spent most of the past decade encouraging students and their teachers to think of writing as a meaning-shaping activity, a way of making thinking visible. Talk, which is audible but invisible enables meaning-shaping of a different kind to take place as do nonverbal media such as music and dance.

From childhood, however, I have enjoyed the fascination of thinking through writing and I hope that I have collected enough "evidence" in this book to convince readers that writing can indeed shape meaning for anyone who is prepared to pick up a pen or switch on a word processor. These young writers are discovering how to make sense of new information, new concepts, past memories, original ideas, in order to arrive at fresh perceptions about themselves and their world. Writing is helping them towards those understandings which are evidence that real learning has taken place.

Acknowledgments

I would like to acknowledge the unstinted co-operation of Gill Clarkson, Sue Dean and Jo Stone—the three indefatigable coordinators of the Wiltshire Writing Project, the support of the Local Authority for which I work, the time that many friends generously gave to read and comment on my first draft, and most of all, the many teaching colleagues and their pupils without whose joint contributions this book could never have been written—with a special acknowledgment to Margaret Jensen, whose thirteen-, fourteen- and seventeen-year-old students produced such thoughtful journals about the literature they were reading in her classes.

A Note to
American Readers

In most cases I have indicated how old pupils are who are the main contributors to this book, but I also use British terminology when referring to particular grades, so here's a conversion table for ready reference. I should add that for British teachers the word "children" can refer to both primary and secondary age pupils.

USA	UK	
Kindergarten	Reception Infants	
Grade 1 (6–7)	Middle/Top Infants	
Grade 2 (7–8)	1st-year Juniors	
Grade 3 (8–9)	2nd-year Juniors	Primary
Grade 4 (9–10)	3rd-year Juniors	
Grade 5 (10–11)	Top Juniors	
Grade 6 (11–12)	1st year	
Grade 7 (12–13)	2nd year	
Grade 8 (13–14)	3rd year	
Grade 9 (14–15)	4th year	Secondary
Grade 10 (15–16)	5th year	
Grade 11 (16–17)	6th year (Lower Sixth)	
Grade 12 (17–18)	7th year (Upper Sixth)	

1

Human Brainpower

Some Basic Capacities

I find it ironic and also sad, that after more than a century of state education, we are still operating with a system that sets out to differentiate our children and young people into the bright, the mediocre, and the bloody awful—or if you prefer a less blunt version, into the "gifted," the "average" and the "special needs" pupils. As a profession we are currently being exhorted, indeed required to evaluate youngsters according to arbitrary and predetermined "levels" of performance and lest we should falter in our task, to look to the tightening of screws on our instruments of measurement.

I am firmly opposed to the notion that human intelligence is quantifiable, and angered at an approach to learning which has the arrogance to claim that it is possible—indeed right and proper, to make so-called objective judgments about the intelligence of others, especially when those "others" are vulnerable children and teenagers. In my view a teacher's goals, both short and long term, should be to find ways of giving all pupils such confidence in their own learning powers, that their motivation to arrive at fresh knowledge and new perceptions is heightened daily.

Paradoxically, I believe that all learners would surpass our current expectations, if we were to spend more time inside our classrooms revealing to them what they are already capable of doing (but take too much for granted to utilize fully)—and demonstrating to them how active and responsive their brains can be, *without exception.* Such an approach would seem to offer a positive alternative to devising ways to sort our students into those who can, those who could with a struggle and those who can't— a sure way of insinuating that we regard the mental equipment of at least two-thirds of the school population as under par or below standard. Even

1

when tests are labeled "diagnostic," they still carry a message of failure for those who are deemed by their testers to require additional help.

It is for these reasons that I offer a "capacity-based" approach to learning, which operates on the assumption that all children possess both the ways and the means of making sense. I offer it as an alternative to a "skill-based" approach, which operates on the assumption that initially children are pretty skill-less and therefore, once they are at school, need to be taught in considerable detail how to go about working with a variety of media (words or paint or metal or music or mathematical symbols) *before* they can shape meaning in a way that is acceptable to their teachers—and beyond teachers, parents; and beyond parents, employers or universities. The degree to which young learners can be encouraged to make sense or to shape meaning *in ways that are satisfactory to themselves* tends to be overlooked if the teacher's stance is based first on training "skills"—and then on measuring them.

Even with the best of intentions, such an approach tends to place the learner in a passive position, waiting to be told. A capacity-based approach on the other hand, because it emphasizes both the *what* and the *how* capacities that the child already possesses, places the learner in the position of confident instigator and meaning-maker and the teacher in the position of partner in a joint meaning-making enterprise.

Ways in Which We Make Sense

I am indebted for the following suggestions to Frank Smith's description in *Writing and the Writer* of how the "learning brain" functions and to his insistence that "it is no more 'normal' for the brain not to be learning than it is for the human musculature as a whole to be limp." It is because I agree wholeheartedly with that view, that I want to invite readers to consider an alternative set of basic "R's" to the traditional three: Reading, Writing and Arithmetic, which you will notice, interestingly confine themselves to literacy and numeracy—and in practice to somewhat limited interpretations of these activities: decoding and encoding for literacy, computation for numeracy.

My alternative R's relate to the basic brainpowers that all human beings (unless they have suffered serious and irremediable brain damage) possess from birth: the power to RETAIN memories of encounters with the world outside the head, the power to RE-COLLECT such memories, the power to arrive at new perceptions by RE-CONSTRUCTING or RE-CREATING how these memories appear to us when we consider them afresh, and subsequently the power to RE-PRESENT our new understandings in a form that after reflection, makes further sense for us.

Retaining

All of us, in common with other creatures, absorb and retain impressions or "memories" of the outside world that we take in through our five senses—impressions of what we see, what we hear, what we taste, touch and smell. The extensive use that humans make of sight and sound increasingly influences how we interpret these experiences of the world outside the head, through the verbalizing and the visualizing powers that the human brain has acquired. I consider how these particular capacities interrelate in Chapter 3. This is not to say however, that our retention of other sensory experiences ceases to have significance for us. Consider for instance how poignantly a whole chain of memories can be clustered around a particular smell. For me the whiff of a certain strong disinfectant immediately evokes a vivid cluster of early nursery school recollections; the pungency of garlic cooking recalls quite a different, but equally meaningful set of memories!

Many of the sensory experiences retained in the brain's memory are retained without conscious effort on our part. Children will recount what they saw on television the previous evening—or what they did six months ago on their summer holidays without anyone saying to them beforehand "Make sure you remember this." I'm not certain whether the brain only retains what its owner actually notices, however fleetingly or "absent-mindedly" ; common sense suggests that we are more *likely* to retain what we have consciously noted although it is quite possible that sensory information is absorbed even while our minds are directed elsewhere. *Retention in itself does not constitute learning however;* it is the significance we begin to draw from our memories, through the application of our other basic R capacities, that invests our lives with meaning.

Re-collecting

In this introductory chapter I am deliberately hyphenating the *verbal* forms of four of these alternative five R's as a reminder that in an important sense, however we arrive at new knowledge and new understandings, the process requires us to draw in some way on those experiences which the brain has already retained. Thus learning is not solely a matter of collecting, constructing, creating and presenting—it is a matter of tying back every new encounter into the sense that we have already made, absorbing, modifying and occasionally shifting our previous perceptions kaleidoscopically as a new concept changes the whole pattern. As CLIS (the Children's Learning in Science Group in the UK) have discovered, if a pupil's own picture of how the world works is ignored, her ability to make sense of someone else's picture, the teacher's or the textbook writer's, is seriously impeded.

There would be little point in possessing an increasingly vast store of retained memories, if we did not possess the capacity to re-collect at least some of them. It is impossible to imagine what our lives would be like if every encounter with the outside world had to be made as if for the first time. Without the capacity to remember, learning would be impossible. Clearly even our chances of survival would diminish considerably!

The frequency with which we encounter (and retain) some experiences, renders the recollections of those experiences easy to the point of spontaneity. Think for instance of a baby coming to know its parents or of knowing which gate to open every time we come home. We call such recollections "recognition"—a rapid matching in the brain of past with present experience that happens so swiftly we rarely notice it. On the occasions when we "half" recognize—let's say someone's face without being able to pin down who it is, where we have seen them before, the context—it is easier to detect how recollection involves a memory search and a matching of past with present.

Many of the recollections that children can be encouraged to make will be personal memories of whose existence they are unaware, until the brain has been activated in some way to "come up" with them. Other recollections more immediately to do with school-based activities will be drawn from experiences that have recently been shared with the teacher and with others in the class—a story read aloud, a video program, a field trip. But in these contexts too, we should be ready to acknowledge an interesting element of uniqueness. Not everyone will re-collect quite the same memories of what went on in quite the same way—unless a worksheet or a test is so rigidly constructed, that it obscures and represses individual differences.

Whatever memories may be called forth, as teachers we need to give children strategies that will help them to use their capacity to re-collect as fully as possible. Some recollections may be spontaneously triggered but others take time—need to be fished for with an appropriate bait. If we think about it introspectively, we know that we can send conscious requests to our brain—from the outside in (or from the top down), that will produce recollections that are relevant to whatever memory search we are intent upon making. Instant "mastermind" recovery is not always possible however, particularly if we are searching for clusters of recollections rather than one-word "answers."

Let me emphasize again that none of us, children included, is in a position to "know what we know" until we are given the opportunity to re-collect what we have retained. It is good that many schools nowadays can provide a rich and interesting environment for their pupils, especially in the early stages of their schooling: live plants and animals, carefully selected and arranged artifacts, attractive books of all kinds, video and computer programs, museum visits and so on. The problem is, we are often so busy in-putting, that adequate time (let alone ample), is rarely offered to children to rediscover what has "sunk in," in order to reflect on it further before they are required to re-present what they have "learned."

Re-constructing

Suppose that children *have* been encouraged to re-collect some of their own retained experience—through talking say, or drawing or writing; they can then begin to do something further with this re-collected information. What they decide to do next will depend partly on the kinds of memories, the number of memories and the complexity of the memories that they have brought forth.

If for instance a teacher invites her pupils at the start of a new topic to brainstorm their individual memories to find out how much they already know about water—or whales or William the Conqueror, these outcomes may well happen: everyone will discover that they already know something about the topic, however fragmentary or minimal that knowledge may be; some individuals will be able to re-collect more than others; those who can call back little, are more likely to come up with questions about what they *don't* know—and if asked to do so, everyone—even the most knowledgeable, can brainstorm questions that could lead to further discoveries.

If the teacher then invites the children to work in pairs or fours to share their recollections with each other and to see whether they can sort them out together, then their capacity to re-construct comes into play. In some respects, mental reconstruction is rather like gathering together as many bits as you can find of a limitless jigsaw (no straight edges to put a boundary on knowledge), with the potential for making a clearer picture as you make connections and piece together what you have at your disposal.

Our capacity to re-construct enables us to be flexible in our understanding of the world, continually adjusting our present knowledge in the light of new experience and making sense of what is unfamiliar in the light of present knowledge. In this respect the jigsaw analogy breaks down because there is no absolute meaning residing in the knowledge we already possess; consequently the picture changes as new perceptions occur. We need perhaps to imagine a jigsaw in which each piece is iridescent and multifaceted!

It is my conviction that learners will be more likely to make a start on this process of reconstruction, if they have been encouraged to re-collect and to share what they already know as a starting point. In this way they are drawing upon their present picture of the world, which already possesses some coherence for them. Their own questions can then lead to further investigations which in turn will enable them to come back with further pieces of information which can then be fitted in to the topic "as they see it." James Britton, in A *Language for Life* describes this process of familiarization as follows:

> In order to accept what is offered when we are told something we have to have somewhere to put it; and having somewhere to put it means that the framework of past knowledge and experience into which it must fit is adequate as a means of interpreting and apprehending it.

Re-creating

I want to distinguish between reconstruction and re-creation by relating our capacity to re-construct, to further reflection about secondhand knowledge, and our capacity to re-create, to further reflection about firsthand knowledge.

"Knowledge" at secondhand that is offered to us on a screen perhaps, or in a book, cannot be absorbed as rapidly nor recalled as readily as our firsthand encounters with the world. Thus our attempts to re-collect unfamiliar information are much more likely to be fragmentary and disjointed than the plankton-rich recall of personal memories. That is why our capacity to *re-construct* has to operate *incrementally,* changing the patterns of our present picture as we add more details to it, while by contrast our capacity to *re-create* has to operate *selectively,* picking out from a welter of detail those features of an experience that still retain significance for us. We gain new understanding of our personal memories from the act not of replication but of re-creation. Learning opportunities in school need to take both capacities into account and to acknowledge their different requirements.

Let me give a couple of brief examples to illustrate the difference as I perceive it: if children are invited to re-collect a *personal* memory—about an accident they once had, say, or a special treat, their act of re-collecting will draw upon multiple memories which are already "webbed" into their own lives. A fresh formulation of those memories will involve a refocusing which may highlight some aspects of the original event more vividly than others. Reflection always provides the talker or writer with an opportunity to re-create an experience differently, partly because in memory it is freed from the minute-by-minute sequentiality of its actual occurrence and partly because the "you now" looking back is different from the "you then" and may therefore perceive what happened differently.

The act of re-collecting *secondhand* knowledge is not thus embedded in personal experience. If I know nothing about the Romans in Britain until my teacher tells me, or takes me to an archeological site or a museum, all that I can do initially, is to pick up fragments of "knowledge" which will then need to be *re-constructed* as further information is acquired so that a more coherent "mosaic" of Romans in Britain can be devised, which may lead to the forming of concepts about how these people influenced the landscape and the lives of those they invaded.

There are also interesting differences between secondhand *informational* experience and secondhand *literary* experience, insofar as the personal memories that we are able to bring to the latter, cannot so readily be brought to the former. I would suggest for instance, that pupils can be "drawn in" to a story more fully than they can be "drawn in" to a textbook account of photosynthesis. Consequently, our responses to literature, whether in print, on the screen or on the stage, are likely to be re-creative at least in part, insofar as the work in question "holds a mirror up" to aspects of human nature with which we are already familiar. Our responses to nonfiction on the other hand are likely to be reconstructive, a slow piecing together of separate items of information as we begin to perceive how they connect one with another.

Re-presenting

Where reproducing suggests making a replica, re-presenting more often suggests "standing for" in the sense that the lantern in Pyramus and Thisbe "doth the horned moon present" or in the sense that a representative is standing in for a particular group. As one of my five R's, I am using the notion of re-presentation more specifically to refer to our ways in which pupils can present the outcomes of what they have learned. After children have either re-constructed or re-created their recollections and hopefully in the process synthesized new knowledge with old, then they need to be given the opportunity to re-present what they have learned—what they now know that they didn't know before. I shall therefore hyphenate my fifth R in its verbal form throughout the book, as a reminder of its intended meaning.

The *medium* that we choose for our representations may be spoken or written language or it may be a nonverbal medium such as paint or clay, musical sounds or mathematical symbols. Writing, to which this book will increasingly address itself, is in this respect, just one of many choices that can be made.

When we offer representations of our experience to others they are often regarded as "products" : pictures, poems, essays, a piece of music, depending on the medium that the meaning-shaper has chosen. This has sometimes led to the mistaken assumption both inside and outside the teaching profession, that if the handling of *the medium itself*, is taught in a skill-based way, pupils will become expert (or at any rate competent) artists, writers, musicians, mathematicians and so on.

What is so misleading about this view of teaching and learning is that it fails to recognize the inseparability of a learner's capacity to re-present (whatever the medium), from those other capacities that precede it: re-collecting, re-constructing and re-creating—which in their turn are insep-arable from the learner's own experiences, retained inside the learner's own head. Understanding how to make further sense of this knowledge requires that the learner utilizes whatever medium she has chosen not for its own sake, but meaningfully for her own purposes. Paradoxically perhaps, as the writers of the Bullock Report, *A Language for Life*, recognized, we develop our ability to handle a particular medium as we strive to shape meaning through it. Practicing the manipulation of medium divorced from meaning can only become a barren exercise which motivates the learner minimally if at all.

2

The Brain in Action

A Multiple Helix of Mental Capacities

In the previous chapter I explained what I understand about the *ways* in which humans make sense of the world, and suggested that it might be helpful for teachers to take a capacity-based approach to the pursuit of learning with children, teenagers or adults in all phases of education, which acknowledges that they are all capable of these basic brainpower Rs: the retention of experience and the subsequent recollection, reconstruction, re-creation and representation of whatever has been retained in order to shape new meaning from it.

I now want to consider the *how*—how does the human brain perform these functions? What further capacities does every learner possess which need to be brought into play if she is to make sense of the world outside her head by using what is inside it to do so?

I want to suggest that all of us continually make use (effortless on some occasions and effortful on others) of a multiple helix of capacities which ceaselessly intermesh throughout our waking lives and frequently even in sleep. We can separate them in theory, by giving each a distinct name but in practice they are inseparable. I am referring to our capacity to think, our capacity to feel, our capacity to do or to perform actions, our capacity to visualize the world both outwardly and inwardly and last but not least, our capacity to verbalize.

James Moffett's model of cellular growth in *Student-Centered Language Arts and Reading, K–13* suggested the helix to me, as I was searching for a similar metaphor that would reflect both the organic and the dynamic inseparability of the "how" capacities involved in learning. In the *Shorter Oxford Dictionary* "helix" is defined as "anything of a spiral or coiled form . . . advancing round an axis." This fits well with the notion that *how* we learn depends upon the constant interaction of these mental activities as they spiral and coil around the axis of evolving meaning. If you imagine the diagram in Figure 2–1 in constant movement (and tucked away inside

8

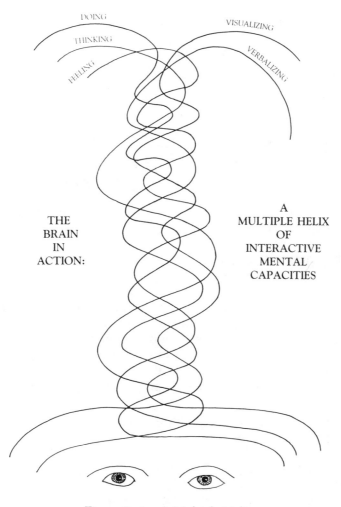

Figure 2–1   A Multiple Helix

that person's head instead of emerging like smoke), then you have the concept of how learning happens that will be useful to keep in mind for the rest of this book. The named strands could come in any order as they continually and inextricably interrelate with each other.

As my focus moves towards an exploration of how the activity of writing can help learners to make sense, I shall be devoting the next chapter to more specific considerations of how our verbal powers are essential to human understanding. In this chapter I want to comment briefly on the other "helical" capacities which make meaning-shaping of any kind possible.

Feeling

The capacity most difficult to define is that of feeling, even though our whole life and everything that happens to us is colored by it. Somehow our feelings appear to be more intangible than actions, words, thoughts and images—and also less convincingly located in the brain. I suspect that we still have the sneaking impression that feelings emanate from the heart rather than the head.

And yet what we make sense of, we always make sense of partly through our feelings, whether these happen to be strongly negative or strongly positive at the time. Every teacher knows how much easier it is to engage a pupil's interest when that child is feeling curious or excited or is eagerly anticipating whatever activity is in prospect. Similarly all teachers recognize the strength of negative feelings such as anxiety and frustration, which make the task of learning doubly difficult if not impossible. Neither are teachers fooled when children say they don't feel anything—"couldn't care less" usually means that they feel vulnerable, uncertain and defensive. Let's face it, if we literally lose our capacity to feel, we become urgent cases for prolonged medical treatment.

In her introduction to the first volume of *Mind: An Essay on Human Feeling* Susanne Langer states:

> The thesis I am about to develop is that man's departure from the normal pattern of animal mentality is a vast and special evolution of feeling in the hominid stock. This deviation from the general balance of functions usually maintained in the complex advances of life is so rich and so intricately detailed that it affects every aspect of our existence, and adds up to the total qualitative difference which sets human nature apart from the rest of the animal kingdom as a mode of being that is typified by language, culture, morality, and consciousness of life and death.

Langer is here clearly regarding the complex development of human feelings as a crucially important aspect of our whole way of interpreting the world, which interrelates fundamentally with all other aspects of our mental development.

The close connections which exist between what we feel, what we think, what we see—and maybe what we do, is also explored, though with tantalizing brevity by Andrew Wilkinson in *The Quality of Writing* (Ch. 5). Wilkinson draws attention to Peters' suggestion (Hurst and Peters, 1970) that the emotions we experience are not "pure" feeling but have a cognitive as well as an affective component, where in the emotional response to another person or to a situation, "the feeling is inseparable from cognition". The example that Wilkinson offers, which involves the *judgment* or the *appraisal* of the person concerned in order for a particular emotion to be recognized as such, is a situation in which "Tom's girlfriend talking sinuously to Dick occasions jealousy in Tom because he appraises the situation as threatening her preference for him. . . . Harry, seeing the same conversation, is indifferent to it and makes no appraisal of it."

Further, it certainly seems to be the case that the motivation to find out more and to reshape what we currently "know" is intimately bound up with how we feel. Who would deny that if we are feeling confident, it is far easier to sustain our efforts to reach a fresh insight than if we are feeling doubtful? In the teaching profession we need to offer strategies therefore which will encourage confidence, and to reject strategies such as formal testing which for many children only serve to increase a fear of failure. The teacher who is willing to work alongside pupils as a partner in the joint enterprise of learning, is more likely to be of educational help than the teacher who is perceived by the pupil as a persistent threat.

Thinking

Thanks to the work of many writers who have been interested in education as philosophers, linguists, psychologists and often great teachers themselves, we are now well aware of the inextricable relationship that exists between our human capacity to verbalize and our capacity to think in a variety of modes—recollective, reflective, analytic, speculative, imaginative. Some of these writers have strongly influenced my own thinking and consequently my classroom practice over the years. I would like to acknowledge a personal debt to the work of James Britton and Ann Berthoff. Both helped me to perceive more clearly how valuable it is for any learner to be able to render thinking audible or visible through the brain's capacity to generate a flow of language. Berthoff puts it like this:

> The tendency of words is to cluster, to form syntactic units. This tendency of words towards syntax is the discursive power of language: syntax brings thought along with it as it runs along.

I shall come back to this interrelationship between verbalizing and thinking in the next chapter, as well as to another intriguing aspect of the brain's capacity to think, which we could perhaps draw attention to rather more clearly when we talk to our pupils about the nature of learning. I refer to the brain's capacity to "make sense" at levels below conscious verbal thought—as though the brain were thinking out of earshot as it were. This is not to deny Vygotsky's proposition that "thought is not merely expressed in words; it comes into existence through them"—rather to suggest that subconsciously words also come into being because the brain has been thinking them into existence.

Listen to how Liam Hudson addresses himself to this question of tacit formulation in Chapter 6 of his book *Human Beings:*

> In looking here at the evidence about conscious and unconscious thought, there are three interpretative points to bear in mind. In the first place, far from being a porridge-like and irrational mess, the mental processes of which we are unaware often prove to possess a high degree of structure. Indeed some of the most precise thinking we do seems to be thinking to which we have little access and over which we exert a minimum of control. Secondly, the distinction between conscious and unconscious is, in any case, far from clear cut. There exist massively influential forms of thinking that are strictly speaking

neither conscious nor unconscious, but *tacit*. And thirdly, our thinking is shaped by our needs.

This blurring of the boundaries between explicit and inexplicit awareness helps me to grasp the distinction that Polanyi and others have made between articulate and inarticulate knowledge. Take for instance, the example of the young child's tacit or intuitive awareness of how her mother tongue operates, while still not able to define the rules which govern its workings. Explicit formulation may be years away, but the brain's capacity to make inward sense is already standing her in good stead.

If we accept, as it seems to me we must, that much of our knowledge is tacit before it becomes explicit, this raises a serious question about the educational validity of testing children by demanding "precise" answers to a series of questions which are not their own in the first place, and then generalizing about how much they "know" on the tenuous evidence provided by their (often bewildered) responses.

Another characteristic of thinking to consider, is its recursive quarrying movement, like a dog chasing an interesting scent. When we think, we try to make connections and see patterns, which will lead us to interpret the significance of whatever it is that we are thinking about in ways that had not occurred to us before. We think analogically, in order to link what is initially strange and puzzling, to points of reference in our previously retained experience which are reassuringly familiar. How else can we reach an understanding which is also an insight? My mother had a saying about progress that "It's one step forwards and two steps back." Thinking is rather like that; if we try to push children too hastily into the acquisition of new knowledge, we shall only be laying in store for them all those negative feelings of confusion, frustration and dismay which only serve to make learning difficult. In order to think forwards we continually have to think back. I suggest that this is as true for speculative and imaginative modes of thought as it is for the analytic and the explanatory.

Visualizing

One of the capacities that children take very much for granted because the brain appears to perform in this way quite effortlessly, is its capacity to re-present the world to its owner, not just in a flow of language but also in a flow of images or pictures. I find this capacity truly amazing, for as Frank Smith ponders in *Writing and the Writer,* how on earth does the brain *do* it? There are no actual pictures forming and reforming in the cells and indeed, as Smith points out, this tireless organism that provides innumerable films of retained experience for us, is never in direct contact with the world that it enables us to "see"—both outside the head and in the mind's eye.

I think it's well worth drawing children's attention to this powerful capacity which they all possess, in order to involve it more fully in the learning process. If we choose to do so we can call up a never-ending stream of visual memories. Indeed it is difficult to imagine how utterly different our recollections would be were there no visual element to them. In the last ten years I have come across just four people out of thousands—two adults and two children—who stoutly and sincerely maintained that they absolutely never saw pictures inside their heads. My hypothesis would be that we must all possess a subconscious visual store of images similar to our tacit store of words, upon which the brain is able to operate outside the range of conscious awareness. Otherwise how could any of us recognize our friends, our foes, and more mundanely, our houses and our cars? Happily most of us can also recall such images consciously into mind.

One of the intriguing differences between images that we see inside our heads and what we look at in the outside world, is the insubstantiality of the introspective view. We can look at a scene outside the window as I am doing now and it stays there for as long as I care to observe it. It takes a greater effort of concentration to hold an image still and to hold it clear when we are looking inwards. Inner images tend to move and to flicker with the same rapidity as inner speech. We can however slow them down and "fix" them rather like developing fluid fixes a photograph, by changing them into words—either spoken or written. More of this when I come to strategies for writing in Chapter 5.

Doing or Enacting

If you ask children what their brains can do they will very often say, "send messages to my arms and legs"—and it's perfectly true that in that biological sense we rely on the brain to govern the complexities of the nervous system. At its most basic, the capacity to perform any physical act relies upon such sensory-motor messages. Undeniably doing is the most overtly physical activity in the helix—doing can make us pant and sweat, it can cause aches and pains, it can involve finely tuned and finely co-ordinated motor movements. In the multiple helix of learning activities however, I am thinking of our capacity to "do" as it intermeshes with one or more of the other mental capacities, as the learner seeks to arrive at some new perception or fresh understanding.

Refining the action, or sequence of actions that the doing involves can in itself become the major goal. All forms of athletic activity spring to mind—along with the appropriate metaphors! Yet even when the improvement of one's own physical performance is uppermost in the learning task, some of the other helical capacities will be involved as well. Imagine a gymnast in training, for instance. Whether she feels confident or tense, this will affect her ability to perform. Her capacity to visualize *inwardly* how a complex sequence of actions is to go, may affect their implementation. She may be offering herself an inner running commentary: "Now keep calm, remember to take off a bit closer to the bar next time, grip with the toes but not too tightly"—and so on.

Certainly where the improvement of physical performance is at the forefront of the learner's mind, bodily actions are paramount—but I would say never in total isolation, whether for individual or for team sports. To learn how to do something better, we also need to visualize, to verbalize, to think and to feel. In this respect "doing" is simultaneously both a physical and a mental experience. On the very day that I came to make a final revision of this chapter, I read the following paragraph in my morning paper:

> "We think in pictures and we think in words" ; John Sayer, sports psychologist, talked gently as he introduced this novel idea to the lads of Queen's Park Rangers. Q.E.D. (BBC 1) had hired him to work with the team for six weeks to improve their mental attitude to the game.

Presumably he was aiming to improve their actual performance on the field by encouraging them to bring *all* their helical capacities into play!

There are of course many learning situations other than sport in which doing is important—such as learning to drive a car or to play a musical instrument or to use a lathe or a paintbrush or a pen. We are more likely to understand the ins and outs of the combustion engine if we have got our hands oily inside the bonnet of a car. We can only get to grips with how to make a computer work for us by having a hands-on experience.

In such instances, doing is an essential component of learning: we can only learn how to do some things by doing them. At the same time, it is important to recognize that we never perform mindlessly if we are aiming to arrive at fresh insights about our performance.

3

Why Verbalizing Is Special

I am giving our capacity to verbalize a chapter of its own, partly because it is such a distinctively human capacity and partly because the chapters which follow will focus predominantly on that particular form of verbalizing that we call writing. A separate chapter must not be taken however, to imply that verbalizing can function independently, any more than doing can—or thinking or feeling or visualizing.

Let me explain why I have chosen to call this capacity our capacity *to verbalize,* and not our capacity *to use language.* It was Neil Postman and Charles Weingartner's book, *Teaching as a Subversive Activity,* which first drew my attention to how calling something a verb-word implies that we are referring to a process whereas calling something a noun-word implies that we are referring to an object. Thus as Berthoff suggests, the word "language" has "thingy" connotations. The implication is that we are referring to the "stuff" or the material out of which we shape our thoughts into telephone calls or speeches or letters or books. The human brain's capacity to generate a comprehensible flow of words, which at the point of utterance creates audible or visible thought, is considerably more complex than a mere "putting into words"—or to use another of Berthoff's analogies, putting the batter of thought into the muffin tray of language. We need to demonstrate to children that they are not just language *users,* they are powerful language *generators.*

In the previous chapter, I reflected briefly on the inextricability of thinking and verbalizing and speculated that even below consciousness, each activity may generate the other. In *Thought and Language,* Lev Vygotsky *p44* hypothesizes that the inner speech that children develop only after they have become fluent talkers, takes on a less syntactic form inside the head, thus enabling thoughts to flow more freely. My problem with this interesting speculation is that I cannot observe it, and therefore cannot investigate it, as I have to slow my thinking down to normal syntax speed before I can hear it clearly.

I am intrigued however, by Vygotsky's suggestion that there are "different phases and planes a thought traverses before it is embodied in words," although I am more inclined to think that there may be different phases and planes of consciousness that thoughts and words traverse *together,* but with shifting emphases and shifting forms. It may be possible for instance, that in some phases of mental activity, inner speech may be too fluid or too fast to be audible, but as we make conscious efforts to catch ourselves thinking, we begin to hear the verbal shape of our thoughts—*especially if our intention is to write our thinking down.* Our overtly spoken thoughts on the other hand, often appear to move directly from unconscious to audible formulation, although to take a constructive part in discussion we need to be aware of the inner dialogue taking place inside our heads as we listen, in order to make a meaningful contribution to the talk. So planes of consciousness there well may be—but continually shifting and sliding into each other as the helix of interrelating capacities spirals through them.

From my own introspection, I can claim as no doubt you can, that although I can only speculate about the existence of a form of inner speech stripped of syntax, I do know that I possess the capacity for conscious inner speaking, which bears a close resemblance to vocal speech. I can listen to my thoughts for quite sustained periods without a word being spoken. Those of you who have to make frequent journeys by car will be familiar with the experience of being so intent upon your own thoughts that there are times when you come to with a start and take a second or two to recognize the landscape on the other side of the windscreen. It is difficult however, to be specific about how far the thinking-out-loud or egocentric monologue stage in childhood overlaps with the development of this silent but nevertheless audible inner speech. When my son was around the age of five, I remember him asking as we were driving along in the car, "What are you thinking Mummy?" after I had been quiet for a matter of minutes. Such a question would suggest that he had by then internalized the notion of inner speech being a form of thinking, because he had actually noticed himself doing it and therefore knew that without actually speaking out loud, someone could be speaking soundlessly inside the head.

What I want to emphasize most from the point of view of teaching and learning, is that whether we are thinking inwardly or aloud, there is a *flow* to the process, sometimes steady, sometimes intermittent. When thinking is consciously happening, it will reveal itself through a running visual sequence of images or a running verbal flow of words. That is why I suggested in Chapter 1 that human learners make increasing use of sight and sound, visualizing and verbalizing. Because we can transpose images into words and words into images, both forms of making and shaping meaning become very important to us in this fluid and interrelated way.

Consider for a moment how children develop their capacity to think in a word-flow. As we all know, a baby's initial exploration of its verbal powers is oral—often very oral indeed! From the babble-music which captures the intonations and rhythms of the mother tongue, discrete words emerge, at first singly and then strung together, which form recognizable and repeatable patterns. Research has established convincingly that all normal young children can think through the spoken form of their mother tongue in all its basic syntactical forms by the age of four or five—not merely imitating the speech of others but generating their own.

By the time five-year-olds come to school, they can already recollect and re-present a great deal of their retained experience through a stream of talk—and increasingly through hearing what they think *to themselves*. It is essential in fact that teachers encourage young children to develop their capacity for audible inner speech by devising strategies that will draw their attention to thinking in it as well as to talking out loud. After all, listening to your own thoughts is just as important as listening to the thoughts of others. I have a strong hunch that never paying attention to hearing yourself think, slows learning down—and makes the move from talk into writing and reading more difficult for some children than it really needs to be.

Most five-year-olds have also developed their capacity to re-present what they already know about their world, through visual symbols—wobbly potato shapes with sticks for arms and legs and circles for eyes, lines radiating from a blob to represent the sun and so on. If teachers offer these children a capacity-based approach to their activities inside the classroom, which acknowledges and allows them to demonstrate what they can already do, even the most "deprived" children, given the opportunity, will reveal what competent meaning-makers they have already become.

I know a reception class teacher who asked her youngsters soon after they had arrived in the school, to draw for her anything they could see in the classroom which they thought had energy in it. Christine, the teacher, was part of a small group of teacher researchers who were interested to find out more about how children systematized the world to themselves, before anyone had told them how to do it and what to look for. These children had received no formal teaching about energy—this invitation to draw, may have been the first time she had actually used the word "energy" with them. Nevertheless, between them they drew pictures which re-presented energy in all its conceivable forms: the sun of course, clothes or trees blowing in the wind, people panting and puffed out, light bulbs, television sets, cookers and so on. They could also talk about their pictures and explain to their teacher when she asked them, why they had drawn a particular object: the sun gives us light, the wind is strong, the people are panting because they have used up all their energy and so on.

Reception and middle infants are quite capable of becoming thoughtful writers and readers as well as drawers and talkers. An increasing number of teachers are now taking a serious interest in strategies that will help young children to make as powerful a use of written language in their own meaning-making as they do of talking and listening. I shall say more in the next chapter about how these children can be encouraged to develop confidently as emergent writers.

A brief comment here on how a capacity-based approach to learning can apply to early reading may be relevant. It is useful to remember that reading is always someone else's writing—or in the case of picture stories, someone else's drawing or painting as well. Thus in one sense the acts of recollection, reconstruction or re-creation and re-presentation have already been accomplished by the authors and illustrators. However, in order to make sense of what she sees as she turns the pages, the young child also has to draw upon her own experience, initially as a response to the pictures, and as her own book-looking and book-talking experience expands, increasingly to the verbal as well as to the visual text—thus becoming a meaning-making reader.

Of course it helps if she is given plenty of opportunities both at home and at school to hear those visible words turned back into audible speech. In this way her brain can absorb and retain the immensely varied rhythms of the written word. Thinking drawn into being through writing has different sound patterns from thinking drawn into being through speech. Children need to hear these new sound patterns through the mediation of other readers, before the brain can retain them as it retains all sensory experiences, thus enabling those rhythms when occasion arises, to be drawn back into their own writing. There may be parallels here for the effective acquisition of reading and writing with the effective acquisition of outer and inner speech.

There is also this interactive relationship between visualizing and verbalizing, which can of course be brought to bear on both visual and verbal forms of representation. Children draw before they write and respond to pictures in books before they respond to words. They can comment on what they see, from simple pointing out ("That's a dog Mummy!") to questions ("Is he the farmer?") to interpretations ("That fox is being naughty isn't he?") to speculations ("I wonder when they'll meet the wicked witch . . ."). Later, when they have listened to a longer text without looking at it, or read a text without pictures, children can equally well be encouraged to perform this transposition in reverse and to focus on the images that they were able to visualize, as they listened or as they read.

We all of us to a very large extent take for granted this astonishing human capacity to generate language—whatever our mother tongue and wherever we happen to live in the world. In *Philosophy in a New Key,* Susanne Langer writes: "Language is, without a doubt, the most momentous and at the same time the most mysterious product of the human mind." She goes on to emphasize and to explore the implications of Sapir's view that "language is primarily a vocal actualization of the tendency to see reality *symbolically."* This suggests to me that our propensity to shape meaning by systematizing and organizing experience into patterns, has been vastly helped along by our capacity to express such perceptions verbally. Perhaps the human brain became an obsessive verbalizer driven by this very compulsion to symbolize and systematize its surroundings. As teachers we should encourage all our pupils to treasure and to cultivate it as one of the greatest gifts of their human inheritance.

4

The Act of Writing

I suggested in the last chapter that the words we use as referents for whatever meaning lies behind them, can in themselves influence our interpretations of the meaning thus conveyed. Thus "language" being a noun form, implies that it refers to some *thing*, whereas "verbalizing" being a verb form, implies that it refers to some *activity*. The word "writing" is interesting in this respect because grammatically it can be interpreted as either a noun or a verb—and sure enough, the expectations that we can bring to what the label "writing" represents, can focus on product or on process.

The diagram in Figure 4–1 gives some indication of how our expectations about writing can vary. You might say that our expectations about countless words can vary, so why make an issue about this one? I think it's important, especially for those of us who are teachers, to be aware as clearly as possible of what we mean, because our interpretation will influence how we approach writing day in, day out, and year after year in our classrooms, across age phases, and across the whole curriculum. The writing we require from our pupils and the ways in which we respond to that writing will in their turn, influence the pupils' expectations and consequently their approach to and performance in writing, possibly for life.

Each of the four interpretations of what writing *is*, as they are represented here, are valid. I am not suggesting that we should consider the options and then make one choice to the exclusion of the other three. On the contrary, I want to argue that we should try to ensure that children and older students experience what it is to write from each of these perspectives, so that they can begin to understand how they interrelate with each other.

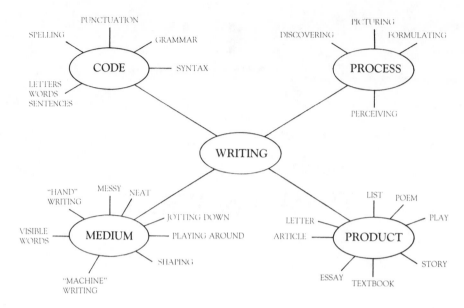

Figure 4–1   Expectations about Writing

Writing Regarded as a Code

The problem is, that some of these expectations or interpretations tend to receive greater attention in the classroom (and therefore greater emphasis) than others. Take CODE for instance. We are all aware whether we happen to be professional educators or not, that learning to write involves learning a whole new symbol system by means of which we transpose a flow of speech sounds into visible letters and punctuation marks, which run across the page or the screen in words, phrases, sentences—and if you are writing prose, in paragraphs. We have to learn how this code works, if we are going to avail ourselves of the power that writing—and reading, can confer.

Naturally therefore, when children first come to school, it is understandable that parents, teachers—and in some cases the children themselves, should be keen to come to grips with the code of written language. The problem is that if the expectation is that writing is about getting the code right *and nothing else,* this can put some children off at a very early stage, especially if they are slow to catch on to the patterns of traditional orthography. If we are not careful, their sense of failure—of being "no good at writing," can become so strong, that they put pen or pencil to paper only with extreme reluctance and thus actually do less and less—which is hardly the way to improve! I know that working on a screen as I am doing now, and being able to erase mistakes at the tap of a key, has gone some way to alleviating the strong disinclination that many children feel about making their thoughts and feelings visible, and I welcome the word processor for that reason alone. But it is not by any means the whole answer to some children's rapidly acquired antipathies.

Writing Regarded as a Medium

These other expectations about the act of writing that we can bring into the classroom to share with our pupils from the start, are probably more important in the long term, with regard to children's views about themselves as writers, and about the usefulness of writing. Take the expectation that writing is a MEDIUM (like paint or clay) that we can make something out of—a kind of verbal play-dough if you like. That "something" will be some aspect of the child's experience that can be re-shaped *and made visible* in the child's own words. It may reach the stage of becoming a finished "product" or it may not. With a new medium, children need to feel that they can play around with it and try things out, without worrying overmuch if their intention doesn't always work out in the way they expect.

I have often wondered why we are so concerned in schools to checklist—or even more off-putting, to test "progress" with such frequency in reading and writing, when other media for self-expression are left well alone. Would it stimulate children to further heights of attainment do you think if they were given painting—or even sand-tray, "ages" ? Surely children should be encouraged to explore and to experiment with this new written medium, just as they experimented with the spoken sounds of their mother tongue from infancy. They can experiment with how meaning takes shape in it and enjoy doing so—if they are given the opportunity, without harassment to respond with the "right" answers.

Later, once they have acquired some familiarity with how to make all kinds of messages on paper out of letters and words, intermingled perhaps with drawings, but most importantly expressing some meaning which is special to them—later, if writing has become meaning full, children will be willing to experiment with this medium as craftspeople such as poets, story writers, speech writers, script writers and journalists do, becoming increasingly aware that meaning is many-layered and that word-changing can effect subtle shifts of sense, as the writer pays close attention to the words that have arrived on the page. They will be fascinated—and sometimes frustrated, by the challenges of a medium which is visible, yet in which meaning must always lie hidden. But unless we bring the expectation to young writers that working with words is a wonderful medium for them to experiment with, too often they are sadly more inclined to regard written language as a straitjacket.

Writing Regarded as a Product

We also need to ensure that all children achieve finished products that give them well-deserved satisfaction. It is our professional responsibility to create the contexts in which such achievements become possible rather than improbable. In the next chapter, I shall be considering the stages of development we can encourage if a potential product is in the making; at this point, let me just quote a cautionary tale, offered by Donald Murray in one of his wise papers about writing in *Learning by Teaching*:

Most of us are trained as English teachers by studying a product: writing. Our critical skills are honed by examining literature, which is finished writing; language as it has been used by authors. And then, fully trained in the autopsy, we go out and are assigned to teach our students to write, to make language live.

Naturally we try to use our training. It's an investment and so we teach writing as a product, focusing our critical attentions on what our students have done, as if they had passed literature in to us. It isn't literature, of course, and we use our skills . . . to prove it.

Our students knew it wasn't literature when they passed it in, and our attack usually does little more than confirm their lack of self-respect for their work and for themselves; we are as frustrated as our students, for conscientious, doggedly responsible, repetitive autopsying doesn't give birth to live writing.

Secondary teachers like myself have a lot to answer for. Because we don't have much time for writing, we forget how long it can take sometimes for the meanings to emerge that we grope towards. We must stop assuming that our pupils can produce finished pieces of literature in the space of two or three weeks, and we must face up to the implications of unreasonably insisting on completed assignments every fortnight. We have to learn how to make more feasible opportunities for serious writing, and how to respond more constructively to such writing as it is taking shape.

At *every* age in our school system I believe we can help children to achieve better products, by giving them more time for the journey that needs to be made, and more help along the way; that goes for five-year-olds as well as for students sixteen and older. We must not at any stage allow ourselves to forget that the act of writing is an act of making sense and of shaping meaning. We should never reduce this act to a product-producing exercise for which the writer has no personal commitment. Nor should we allow ourselves at any grade/age level to pay more attention to the surface features of the product than to the meaning which lies within and behind those features. As teachers, we need to retrain ourselves so that we can look *through* words on a page before we look *at* them.

Writing Regarded as an Active Process

We have considered so far the implications of coming into the classroom with three of the four expectations depicted on my diagram uppermost in our minds. Certainly we want to encourage pupils to become confident CODE breakers, interested in how the MEDIUM of written language can be handled—and proud possessors of many finished PRODUCTS. I would hold these goals in mind for all my students, so-called slow learners included. But unless we also enter our classrooms fully aware of the fourth expectation, I do not believe that pupils will ever fulfill the other three as well as they might otherwise do.

Above all, writing is an ACTIVITY. It is what happens *inside our heads* as we grasp our pen or tap the keys. *Doing* it makes thoughts, feelings and all kinds of recollections visible for us. In that sense, as the poet William Stafford has described, "Writing is a process of discovery." It is also a process of *re*-discovery—a powerful means of attracting into consciousness retained experience that has already undergone some reprocessing in the inner recesses of the mind.

Ironically, it is this *process* expectation about what writing is, and what writing can enable the writer to do, that until recently has been least in evidence in the classrooms of schools and colleges, although without it none of the other expectations can come to full fruition. To me, it is the strongest reason for insisting that writing can be a powerful meaning-shaper for every child, including those whose handling of the code is uncertain, and handling of the medium messy. Specifying such trivia as form filling and formal letters as good reasons for writing, pales into insignificance, compared to the opportunity that writing offers each one of us, to make contact with much that has been happening inside our own heads—and much that can still happen, once we start to re-collect, re-create and re-construct.

Emergent Writers, Emergent Writing

"Emergent" is an expression that is applicable in two important senses to a young child's developing grasp of this strange new activity. In one sense it applies to her developing grasp of the *code* of written language but in another important sense it refers to this developing perception of how meaning can be transferred from the head to the page or the screen *as it takes shape through the movement of the pen or the tapping of fingers.* Because young children are already able to shape meaning through talk, and to some extent through inner speech, we have to understand that the first marks which they make on paper and call writing, can encapsulate what they are muttering, or what they are hearing inside their heads—however indecipherable those marks may be to another reader. These children are not scribble-*thinking* when they scribble-*write*; on the contrary, they are thinking quite fluently in the verbal modes they already possess.

Gradually, as their understanding increases of how the code works, there will be a rapprochement between what they murmur to themselves outwardly or inwardly and how they mark it down, so that readers other than themselves will be able to decode their personal script without their help. Conversely, as these same children develop as readers, *they* will be able progressively to decode what other writers have written.

What we must avoid in school at all costs, with regard to both writing and reading, is any approach which denies children the possibility of *shaping their own meaning* from the very start. Conscientious efforts to give children plenty of practice, learning the code *first*, only serve to confuse, where they were intended to simplify, because the child is being required apparently, to learn the code for its own sake and not as a powerful mode of expression for his own thoughts, feelings and recollections.

I would argue that emergent *encoding* is more likely to develop steadily towards traditional orthography, if the teacher encourages the young writer to mark down what she thinks and feels and remembers in her own version of "writing" from her first day in any classroom. Paradoxically (though logically perhaps when you consider the proposition), this early version of what writing looks like may well carry more meaning for the child than her laborious underwriting of a sentence, which the teacher has correctly transcribed in a code that is still quite foreign and strange to the copier. Her emergent version will also flow faster than a slow copying, which involves many unfamiliar letter shapes; in producing her own writing, the young child will not be distracted from the meaning in her mind; in copying an unfamiliar script, she is likely to lose sight of the meaning altogether, as her focal awareness fastens on letter shapes and sizes. Many researchers have now shown how young children will move with confidence from pre-phonic scribing, through increasingly inventive phonic scribing, to that mixture of phonic and non-phonic which characterizes standard written English, without needing the doubtful prop of exercise copying at all.

This is not to suggest that it is improper for infant teachers or indeed any teachers to draw their pupils' attention to how letters, words and longer blocks of writing are transcribed. As Rudolf Flesch pointed out at some length in *Why Johnny Can't Read,* it is absurd to withhold information from children about the sound/symbol patterns that the written forms of English and American share (approximately!) in common. It is much more a question of when, rather than whether. When a child is working out her thoughts, i.e., *composing,* to insist that she simultaneously try to work out the correct *transcription* can only act as an unwelcome constraint.

There are plenty of opportunities when the child is neither writing nor reading for meaning, when word games can be encouraged which match pictures to letters and letters to sounds, and which encourage the players to build letters into words and words into sentences. Children are often keen code-breakers and want to find out how the code of writing works—especially if their emerging sense of its heuristic possibilities is given every chance to grow, alongside their emerging understanding of its form.

I have a strong hunch however, that if children are encouraged to compose and to construe for meaning from the start, the time they will need to spend on language games will decrease. We need further research evidence from teachers who are encouraging emergent writers and readers: case histories which reveal how literacy development occurs when the writer or reader is confidently "in charge."

Sheila Fitzgerald, Professor of Education at Michigan State University, has introduced me to another interesting possibility. Why not use singing she suggests, as a vocal and strongly rhythmic mode of expression, which can form a helpful bridge between speech and writing. When children learn a nursery rhyme or a song (Fitzgerald instances "I'm a little teapot" and "The farmer's in his den"), they learn the words and the tune together. Often they may accompany their chanting with actions, thus bringing another helical capacity into play! As I read Fitzgerald's article, I was taken back to song games I played as a small child such as "Here we go Luby Loo" and "Here we come gathering nuts in May" and to skipping songs such as "Jelly on the plate! Jelly on the plate! Wibble wobble, wibble wobble, Jelly on the plate!"

Often children never see these songs and games written down. Fitzgerald's point is that if children are encouraged to use their own discovery writing to "make a song book," they will do so with confidence because *they already have the words and the rhythms ringing in their ears.* In their own time they can match their versions with the versions that they then see in books or on song sheets. The teacher can also invite children to pick out key words from a favorite song presented to them in print, as a collaborative word game in which all can join.

A teacher who encourages emergent writing, is likely to encourage emergent reading too. Like talking and listening, reading and writing are two sides of the same coin. After all, reading *is* someone else's writing although children may not realize this until it is pointed out to them. One of the most powerful ways of encouraging youngsters to become writers is to encourage them to become readers. What more effective way of allowing the realization to dawn, about how words *look* when thinking becomes visible—by just as importantly demonstrating how written words *sound* as they come off the page.

Composition in writing is interestingly different from composition in speech; it has its own special—and immensely varied, rhythms. It is essential therefore, that children hear purposeful writing of all kinds read aloud, if their brains are to be given the opportunity of enriching their own store of retained experience about how writing *sounds*. How else are they to acquire a sense of the possibilities that writing can offer to confident meaning-makers as they listen to their thoughts taking shape?

One last word about emergent writers writing. It may be that some children will never master all the intricacies of traditional orthography—after all, how many of us could claim that we never spell a word incorrectly? So, shaky spellers some may remain. But if we could only remove the stigma that attaches to erratic spelling by placing greater emphasis on the meaning that lies within the words, responding to that emerging meaning wherever it is apparent, perhaps we could convince more children that writing can become an exciting act of discovery and a powerful mode of expression.

5

Writing Journeys—
Some Traveling Strategies

We need to free our pupils from the assumption that the minute words are written down, they somehow fix meaning forever, like a fly in amber. Essentially thinking and verbalizing are interactive mental processes that flow. We can hear this in talk because speech moves through time but once words are left on the page they acquire an immobility that can easily have a petrifying effect. This can prevent children from regarding writing as anything other than an extremely intransigent medium which they dislike using and are reluctant to tamper with once words are inscribed in it. The ease and rapidity with which these marks can be wiped off the word-processing screen is helping to reduce this sense of fixity, but simply changing from handwriting to machine-writing will not ensure the fundamental change in attitude that is essential if writing is to empower more youngsters to become meaning-shapers.

Teachers need constantly to emphasize to their pupils that writing is an ACTIVITY—a powerful MEANS of making sense, a PROCESS which will help them to recollect, to re-create, to reconstruct and re-present. Teachers need to let their pupils know that they are also aware that it *takes time* to shape new meaning, to move from the retention of new information to an understanding of its significance, to create a story from beginning to end, to work on a poem until you're satisfied with the way it looks and sounds, to respond insightfully to another writer's work. If writing is chosen as the mode of expression that accompanies the learner's learning, then it seems sensible to assume that the writing too needs to perform different functions as the writer explores new ground.

As Figure 5–1 indicates, I find the metaphor of a journey applicable in many respects to writing as a learning process. All journeys take time, and when the going is tough some will take longer than others. It is possible on a journey to have a rest along the way—several rests, if the journey is an extended trek over unfamiliar ground. It is possible to look back over

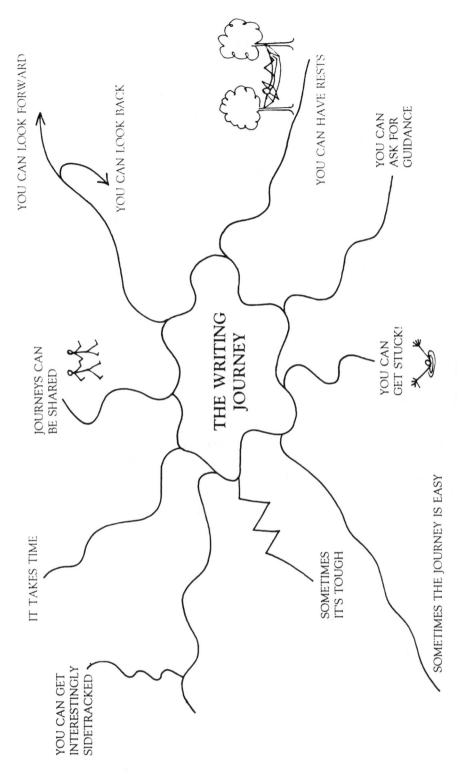

Figure 5–1 The Writing Journey

ground already covered and to look forward at least as far as the next bend. It is useful to be able to call on help if you get stuck, and it can be reassuring to have company at least from time to time, as the journey progresses. I don't want to press these analogies too closely, but all have relevance to the learner-writer and may help her to keep going—especially in the face of difficulties.

All too often, the experience of young writers in school can be both lonely and threatening to their self-confidence and self-esteem. All too often, their teachers can come to be regarded not as helpful companions but as judges, waiting stopwatch in hand at the finish line, to assess their students' unaided performance before starting them off on the next trial run. Where the dominant expectation about writing is code-oriented, this assessment of performance will be perceived as being concerned largely with correctness and hardly at all with making sense. Where "guidelines" such as the following are put forward, this view will be both confirmed and compounded:

> Writing objectives at age seven:
>   Write legibly; use a wide range of simple vocabulary; construct sentences in simple syntax with a fair degree of correctness; use full stops and capital letters accurately; spell correctly any words belonging to simple vocabulary.

So, keeping in mind the reflection that writing which is setting out to shape meaning, is in many respects more like a hike than a hurdle race, this chapter will describe the different functions that writing can take on as the journey proceeds, and make some suggestions about the kinds of responses from the teacher and fellow members of the class that may be of help to the writer, particularly in the early stages of any new undertaking.

Setting Out: Strategies for Getting Started

What is still not always realized, by many primary and secondary teachers, is that a first, continuous draft is often improved enormously, if the intending writer allows herself an exploratory stage first—and is encouraged by her teacher to make a few preliminary sorties that may produce some interesting memories from which further possibilities may emerge. The expectation should be uppermost that writing can be an exciting— and sometimes unpredictable process of discovery. At this initial stage the writer is chiefly engaged in the act of recollection; rather like a beachcomber, she must keep an open mind, an expectant ear and a wandering eye. She must learn how to make a journey inwards before the outward journey can begin. In *Write to Learn* Donald Murray describes this point of departure for the intending writer as follows:

When most people think of writing, they see words on a page, all neatly ordered, marching towards meaning. When writers think of writing, they see a blank page, and they see what was before the blank page. . . . Before I could find words to put on the paper I had to go back. Staring out the window beyond the pile of blank paper, I heard my Uncle Will reciting poems as he carried me in his arms late at night. My grandmother, stern matriarch of our clan, stood approving in the shadows. Do I remember it, or was it something that was told me? No matter, I hear his voice, see Grandma's approving smile, and hear the music of those Scottish poems. Looking out the window in my office I see myself, a small boy in bed, a lonely boy in a house of grownups with problems he couldn't understand. And I remember the stories that boy told himself about football, and fights in the street, and traveling across the ocean, and girls. There were more and more stories about girls.

What has this got to do with this book? Everything. That's where it started. The boy had learned to read and write, and the excitement in writing was that he didn't know exactly what he was going to say when he wrote. There were always surprises on the page. Sometimes the surprises were large, sometimes small, but there was always something unexpected.

So how can we help our pupils, confronted with the blankness of a sheet of paper, to see beyond it into that rich terrain of retained experience stored inside each head? We need to find ways of demonstrating that everyone's brain is both packed with memories and capable of responding to requests for specific recollections. Here the familiarity of today's children with computers comes in handy. They know that computers have "memories" that can be programmed to search for specific information. There is no difficulty in suggesting that our brains function in a similar way, and a short step from that suggestion is to invite them to try out a few instructions on their own "mental computer" to find out what happens when they set a memory search of their own in train.

Brainstorming for Information

In this context, brainstorming, as I am using the expression, means not so much a lateral thinking free-for-all, as a series of focal messages or requests, which are consciously "fed in" to the intending writer's head, with the firm expectation that the brain's capacity to recollect will immediately be activated. We can all brainstorm for facts, for feelings, for questions, for ideas, for personal memories; we can also consciously utilize the brain's verbalizing and visualizing capacities to brainstorm for images and words.

The simplest form of brainstorming is to request that the brain come up with a list of names—place names, birds' names, names of games, whatever. Have the class program one such directive into their own heads, then give them just sixty seconds to see how many names they can recollect. The brainstorm can be thinking out loud (but then the words have disappeared into thin air so that you can't check how many names you actually thought of), or thinking silently (but the names tend to word-wrap themselves back out of conscious memory), or jotted down on the blank sheet as they come to mind. This demonstrates to brainstormers how useful writing can be as a way of making thoughts visible. When I work with children I always make it clear that as long as they can read their own writing, that is all that is necessary at this stage; it doesn't have to be neat, it doesn't have to be correct, as long as it begins to fill up that blank page with possibilities.

When children have taken a minute to jot names down, I invite them to share their lists with a partner and to add any further names that may occur to them as they swap ideas. Collaborative recollecting will pave the way for collaborative reconstructing—and later on for collaborative revision. Pupils also enjoy this fairly rapid shuttling back and forth between writing and talking, as it provides company from the outset.

Once there is a written list, however short, there is always more that can be done with it. Let's suppose that we have a list of birds' names. The class can now be invited to underline the name of the bird each of them thinks they know most about—and then to do another brainstorm to rediscover exactly what they *do* know. They can be told to write this second list just as they hear it inside their heads, as the brain's memory search takes place—in single words, perhaps, or in word clusters, or in whole sentences. Supposing I had underlined "robin" on my list. In the five or six minutes allowed for this more extended search I might jot down

> Has a red breast, very thin legs, bright round eyes, a tiny pointed beak, mouse-brown wings. A Christmas bird. Male robins have their own, fiercely guarded territory. Someone called David Lack wrote a book about robins. They are inquisitive and unafraid of humans— perch on spade handles etc.

This would probably have been written down the page, without punctuation, if I had been scribbling onto a piece of paper. Again, these recovered memories can be exchanged, with a partner or more generally around the class as a whole. It is important to remind everyone that writing is a very useful way of recollecting or rediscovering what we already know, so that this recovered knowledge can be shared with others and talked about some more before it is taken any further in writing.

At the start of a new topic—be it in English or humanities or science or maths, it is always helpful to invite the group to find out *what they know between them already*, before moving into a fresh investigation; in this way what is already familiar is established in order to provide that "somewhere to put it" framework, that Britton claims is essential for the successful grafting on of new facts, new concepts, new ideas.

Brainstorming for Questions

Suppose we are about to spend the next three or four weeks finding out more about birds. After at least some of the class's current knowledge has been rediscovered in this way, it is then useful to brainstorm for questions which focus on what the children *don't* know about the topic. I might at this stage write down:

> What is the difference between the English robin and the American robin? Are they the same species? How many different species of birds are there—a) in the British Isles? b) in the world? How long do birds live? Does this vary from species to species? Do some kinds of birds live longer than other kinds? Are different human races the same thing as different bird species? Why do birds migrate? How do they know where to go? How come they can find exactly the same spot every year at each end of a thousand mile journey?

Those questions are all genuine questions for me. It took me a couple of minutes to type them into the word processor. I didn't know what they would be until I allowed the brainstorm to suggest them to me.

Given encouragement, children have no problems coming up with their own questions. Remember that eager spirit of enquiry that talkative four-year-olds show—that constant battery of questions ("Why does the sun stay up in the sky Mummy?") which their exhausted parents very often can't answer? Well, schoolchildren and even university students are perfectly capable of brainstorming for their own questions, if "shades of the prison house" have not prevented them from doing so. Given the bird topic by a colleague of mine, a small group of six- to seven-year-olds produced these robin questions:

> Why do robins like winter? How did the robin get its name? What other colors are there on its body? What color is a young robin? Where do you often see them? What do they eat?

Collect the two "best" questions from every child in the class, write them across the display board on the back wall, and you have a program of mini-investigations which can take as much or as little time as you or the class want to spend. The children choose their first "I-search" question (to use Ken Macrorie's apt phrase) from this common bank of possibilities and set off to see what they can find—in the library, from the special project collection, from pictures as well as text, from television programs perhaps, from other people. If they can find no further information in response to one question, then they register that it remains a mystery question and choose another one from the pool.

When the children come to share what they have found out, and to work out how they can re-present it, then they will be involved in the process of reconstruction that "changes the jigsaw," and extends the network of their knowledge. This will still vary of course from child to child, depending on how much they know already and on how successful their various I-search quests have been. Hopefully everyone, including the teacher, will know more at the end than they did when they started. Most important of all, the "conclusion" of any investigation should also recognize that there are still many more questions to be asked—always, whatever the topic, there is scope for further enquiry.

In *Writing and the Writer*, Frank Smith comments:

> I do not know why we are so reluctant to acknowledge mystery, especially since the world seems so full of it in so many ways. Children are rarely taught about mystery, although I am sure they understand and respect it. Instead, we encourage them to believe that only knowledge exists. The educated person knows everything that it is necessary to know, or at least knows where to look it up. Why do we associate ignorance with stupidity and value dogma over doubt?

I have a clear memory of Leslie Jackman, a British marine biologist, taking a group of teachers down to some rock pools on the Devon coast and telling us that whenever he worked with children, he always shared a genuine mystery with them before helping them to discover all kinds of life beneath the seaweed. Like Frank Smith, he believed that it is what there is yet to discover that stimulates the traveler to continue the journey. I have remembered the mystery that he shared with us that day, although many of the technical names for the plants and the sea creatures that we saw have slipped away: "When limpets float off the indentation that they make on a rock face to feed, they always return to that identical circle. They are simple creatures and shouldn't be able to do this and yet they do! No one yet knows how."

Brainstorming for Personal Memories

So far I have described how any class can be invited to brainstorm for information in order to rediscover what they already know and to formulate questions that could lead to new knowledge. But if we so choose, we can also brainstorm for feelings, for personal memories, for images, and for ideas. Often of course there will be an overlap—personal memories are colored by feelings which can be vividly recollected, and frequently they are strongly visual. Thus, to go back to our list of birds' names, instead of being asked to underline the bird they think they know most about, pupils could be invited to look down their list and underline any bird that brought a personal memory to mind, or a bird that for whatever reason they had strong feelings about, or the bird they could picture most vividly inside their heads. It helps initially if everyone in the group focuses their memory search in the same way personal feelings or visual images or recollected information—so that what they remembered doing or feeling or seeing can be shared from some common ground. It's a good demonstration of the uniqueness and the fertility of everyone's memories, because although the "message" given to everyone's brain has been the same, what emerges is always richly varied.

I know a teacher who encourages her reception infants in their first term to brainstorm out loud. On the occasions when she has a helper who can work with the half dozen or so who find concentration most difficult,

Marguerite can take the rest onto the carpet for a sharing session in which she acts as their scribe. She will introduce a topic and invite the children to tell in turn what they can see—or feel or hear—inside their heads. She writes down every child's offering on a pad in front of her—and keeps circling round the group to find out what second thoughts have arisen for each child, drawn to accompany their first contribution. It has proved to be an effective way of encouraging the children to shape at the point of utterance, not "all-in-one-go" but cumulatively, with mulling-over time in between one suggestion and the next:

> I scribbled Anna's first line on the pad in my hand, and her voice trailed away as she listened to the others. Then . . . "Anna, what you said first was, 'Water goes down the drainpipe' " . . . No response . . . "How?" Anna in a terse voice—"gurgling like frogs when they puff up their chins."
>
> These lines were read back to Anna, but a shake of the head in response to my expectant look made me move on to another child. When I came back to Anna however, a few moments later, and reread them, I had an immediate response:
>
> Anna—"It drips down the plughole." She then gave me a frowning look.
>
> Teacher—"Where does it go?"
>
> Anna—"To the sewer below."
>
> Teacher—"Now I'll read what you've said so far:
>
>> Water goes down the drainpipe
>> Gurgling like frogs
>> When they puff up their chins.
>> It drips down the plughole
>> To the sewer below . . . "

A firm shake of the head was her reply, but a few moments later she caught my eye, and again in a very terse manner said: "Out of sight as it goes in."

I then read it all back to Anna, who nodded satisfyingly. "I think it's good," she said. "So do I," I replied. "I do like the bit about the frog's chins," said Elizabeth. "Yes, it sounds like when they turn on the tap next door, and the ghost gets in our pipes," said Clare.

Words into Images, Images into Words

In Chapters 2 and 3, when I was considering the helical capacities of the human brain, by means of which we continually revise our present understandings, I commented on the interrelationship that frequently exists between verbalizing and visualizing. It seems to me that we should be able to offer children strategies, that will both demonstrate and at the same time utilize these capacities, in this exploratory stage of meaning-shaping. Let me describe two ideas that have proved to be successful with all age groups from infants to adults.

Instant Pictures

To work best, this idea and the one that follows need to be presented in the context of "brainpower basics" : finding out what your brain can do is the first goal; if this happens to produce material which provides a starting point for writing, so much the better!

Have the group that you are working with consider how easily we can think in words *or* think in pictures. Ask how many of them can call up an instant picture, inside their head, behind their eyes, of their cat or their dog—or someone else's cat or dog that they know well. Approach the activity as an experiment—waiting to see what will happen if this particular request is telegraphed to the brain. Keeping eyes closed for a few seconds to black out the classroom often helps concentration and the sense of taking part in a joint effort of discovery.

Children are eager to volunteer the picture their brain flashed up— and naturally they tell what they saw in words. The rest of the group can be encouraged to ask questions that will help *them* to see someone else's picture more clearly. The child whose internal image is under discussion discovers that she can always tell more: "Is your dog lying down?" "Has he got his head on his paws?" "What shape are his ears?" This gives children confidence that they can always "fill in the details" and it shows how they can help each other to do so.

After a few more experiments ("What would you see if you were standing looking out of your kitchen/bedroom window at this very moment?" "Who can call up a picture of the place they stayed for a holiday last summer?") which are shared immediately in talk, the class is ready to move on to exploratory writing—jotting down what they see, writing *fast* to catch all the details before they share. Tell everyone that they are now going to use their brains like instamatic cameras to take a single-frame snapshot in response to the single word that you are about to utter.

After the oral warm up everyone should be feeling confident and relaxed; they have all just proved to themselves that their brains can think in pictures and can think in words. Easy peasy! So with luck they will all be ready to have a go at this slightly different variation. I ask them to close their eyes so that they are ready for "the word"—after a second's silence I might then say "castle" or "fairground" or "fire" or. . . . One by one, eyes open and hands start to move across the page. The oral sharing will have highlighted the importance of catching every detail.

This first written picture might take five or six minutes to complete, depending on the age of the group and the speed with which they write. The teacher will write too, to show that she is equally interested and prepared to transcribe the secret picture that is present in her mind's eye. The writing may be in phrases or sentences depending on how the writer has heard her thoughts taking verbal shape as she focused on the frozen image. Sometimes the image turns out not to be frozen but moving, more of a film than a snapshot. This is fine; the activity is not intended to be prescriptive, rather to reveal to children their visualizing and verbalizing powers whatever form these take.

Here are just a handful of written responses from a class of ten- to eleven-year-olds, working in the way that I have just described for the first time:

Umbrella

What I can see is my mums yellow umbrella in the porch and the door mat and the lemon plant in the corna of the portch, and the car outside and that is green. (Nicky)

An old woman with an umbrella in her hand walking past a hard where store. The umbrella is red and white striped with a wooden handle. (Sam)

Conkers

A boy throwing a stick in to the tree and 3 conkers falling down and craking open when they hit the ground. The boy had a red jumper and faded jeans the boy ran up to the conkers and picked them they were big ones he put them in a Sainsburys bag then I can see him getting on his bike and riding away. (Roger)

What I can see in my head is two children playing concors on the playground and one of them just smashed the other one's concor and that person is very upset because that was his last concor. (Gary)

Swans

The Bright feathery swans drifting through the water nice and slow and calmly, with the background of long fine grass, in the evening sunset, with the trees surrounding the lake except from the front or back which was just a long lake going on and on. (Sagib)

I can see two big swans. One is white the other a creamy color. The cream one is the father the other the mother. They have 4 cygnets. One of them is very small alot smaller than the other. They all look as if they are about 2 days old. Around them is water. The banks either side have reeds. In amongst the reeds I can see the swans nest. The sun is shining and there is a small breeze blowing through the trees. The sky is blue and not a cloud in sight. (Vicky)

Three big swans swimming on a pond. There is long grass and bullrushes round the pond and trees and a cottage in the distance. (Lara)

Mental Teleporting

This second idea is really just a variation on "Instant Pictures" and arises naturally out of it. As soon as a child shares a moving picture with the class ("I saw two boys playing conkers, taking it in turns to have a smash at each other"), you can point out that our brains will operate like a film camera just as readily as an instamatic; they can run off whole sequences of pictures for us—rather like watching our own private television screen inside our head. Explain about mental teleporting: how although we can't physically teleport ourselves to other planets at the speed of light, we can all do the next best thing, which is to teleport ourselves elsewhere inside our heads.

If it's pouring down outside and the classroom windows are all steamed up, suggest that everyone rest their head on their arms, or just sit back comfortably, eyes closed, and teleport themselves to the seaside. Ask everyone just to stand still wherever they have landed in this internal landscape, and to focus on what they can see in their immediate vicinity. Pause, eyes open for a minute or two to jot this down, eyes closed again. Ask everyone, wherever they may be, to look around now, to the far horizon—and to write down the details. Ask if they can actually hear any sounds inside their heads; ask them to write down what their thoughts are as they survey the scene. Finally ask them to start walking in whatever direction they like and to jot down what else they notice as they go along.

There are many variations to this strategy—and to the places a group can be invited to visit. I have teleported groups to the entrance to their local supermarket, and thence to a walk round the shelves ("What do you see as you start to push your trolley up the first aisle? What are you thinking?"), to the entrance of a tunnel prior to a walk along it, into a lift, into a hospital, to the foot of a dark flight of stairs, onto the drawbridge of a castle and to many more places.

What you are providing in the early stages of working with a group by means of this "guided teleporting" is a collection of possibilities, from which everyone can pick and choose. These short bursts of writing in response to open questions or suggestions—such as "What do you see?" "Now start to move forwards," may turn out to contain ideas for what will later be written in a continuous draft. For this reason I encourage both primary and secondary pupils to think of all their writing in this exploratory stage as "compost" writing. It's not the words themselves or the order of the words on the page that matter; it's the seeds of possibilities *which lie behind them.*

Let me illustrate the point with an example that has worked well with primary and secondary pupils—and on several occasions with adults too. The group is asked first of all to take a minute to brainstorm a list of as many kinds of doors as they can think of—cage door, lift door, trap door, car door and so on.

They share with a partner and add any further doors which they fancy to their own list. They are then asked to run their eyes down this extended list in order to decide which of those doors they can see most clearly in their mind—along with a bit of whatever the door is attached to (doors not tending to float about in space).

This leads to a five- to ten-minute free write from everybody—including the teacher, or possibly a drawing followed by a free write. The teacher then asks everyone to decide whether they are on the outside or the inside of their door, allows a few seconds for this silent decision to be made, and then announces that someone—or something, is about to come through their door from the other side. Another five- to ten-minute free write follows. In this way, children have begun that process of recollection and re-creation that they will need to explore further when they come to choose a more extended form for their first draft.

On one such occasion I chose a wardrobe door from my list. I had asked the class to make a drawing of the door they could picture most clearly, and I drew a rough sketch of my wardrobe image while they were drawing their doors. While the children wrote about the door they could picture most clearly, I wrote:

> I see a very large old mahogany wardrobe—big enough to have a person stand up in it—or even two people! The double doors both have very ornate elaborate keys which stick out from the lock and glint like gold. One door has a long mirror set into it which reflects bits of the room—the corner of a bed, and a window which must be set into the opposite wall. The light is dim and the wardrobe is somehow threatening as its great bulk looms up in the gathering shadows.

I knew by the time I had written this, that this wardrobe was providing me with the potential for a gripping story. After we had shared our thoughts about our drawings in pairs, when the time came for the next five-minute free write about who or what was coming through the door, I had no problem getting started:

> I had my back to the wardrobe because I was looking through the window at the gathering gloom of the long empty street. Then I heard a kind of creak in the room behind me and as I turned round to discover what it was, I saw the door of the old antique wardrobe that my aunt had recently left me slowly swing open.
>
> I had thought both doors were locked so I was somewhat taken aback to see what was happening. Then I froze into petrified stillness as what seemed a dark shadow—darker than the air around it, slowly oozed out of the half open door and spread out like smoke across the room towards me.

The lesson came to an end but I have kept my drawing and these two exploratory bits of writing because I have the feeling that they contain the seeds of a story still waiting to be written.

Visualizing a Text

Just as we can change images into words, so we can change words into images. Children or indeed older students, can be invited to focus on making a specifically visual response to a text—a short story perhaps or a poem (as they listen to it read aloud or read it silently for themselves). In other words they program their brains to picture-think while they are listening or reading but then, immediately afterwards, they write down whatever they envisioned or imagined most clearly. If the text makes a powerful impression, the writing which follows often has a strongly rhythmic quality, as well as capturing the feelings that the reader is bringing to the text along with the images. Here is what Derek wrote in the space of about ten minutes after he had listened to *The Highwayman* by Alfred Noyes:

He moves his black gloved hand up to the old inn window. He got his old many-used red whip out and knocked quietly on the window with the red many times used whip. She opened up the shutters and looked at him with her dark black eyes while she was plaiting love plaits in her hair.

The ostler possessed by the maddened Devil listens carefully to (what) the (old greybearded) highwayman. Now this old man loves the landlord's daughter like he loves drinking. He gets maddened by the words of love, and jealousy takes over. The small disfigured humble man shuffles out the back going down the hoof pressed hill, down past the trees where many have been hanged for murder and dishonest deeds, down past the old rivers where many a fish has swam, into the old war site towards the old redcoats offices where wax drips off the candles.

A ten-year-old girl in the same class wrote:

I saw a highwayman riding quickly towards an inn with the wind howling silently round him. Then a gunshot rang through the air and the highwayman was thrown off his horse and lay on the cobbled road, still. The pools of his own dark red blood mixing with the beautiful red of his cloak making a dark purple color. The lacey collar he wore was no longer white but a deep scarlet. His white horse galloped far over the hill. As the rain began to fall the blood mixed with the rain. His pure white mare far away now was spattered with blood. Not far away from the highwayman is an old inn. Inside was the highwaymans love, the innkeeper's daughter, shot dead, still gagged and tied with a musket to her chest on the floor in puddles of her blood. The musket, once a bright, shining silver is now a metallic red. As midnight comes two spirits rise, one from each body and meet in the road. They walk together hand-in-hand to the inn.

Depicting Thoughts and Feelings

In the exploratory search for meaning, it is sometimes helpful to make a start with some form of nonverbal representation as a way of drawing ideas together. The notion is naive that after infancy, drawing need only serve writers as illustration; so of course is the notion that pictures in stories carry only slender meaning for the competent decoder. Meaning can be shaped and carried through the act of drawing and painting just as powerfully as it can be shaped and carried in words.

A picture map of a remembered journey—made in real life or made through someone else's story, can provide an initial reconstruction that free writing and drafting can then explore further. A sketch of a place, or a face, can draw out for the writer what she feels and thinks about that character or that environment. Drawing from direct observation—a leaf, a shell, a hand, a squashed coke tin—can focus attention on features of the object under scrutiny that might otherwise have gone unnoticed, at the same time calling forth other ideas and memories associated with it that the drawing-time has allowed for.

Free writing which follows drawing needs to be taken "at a run" to catch whatever thoughts became a silent accompaniment to the sketching; or key words that are going to be important for the drafting stage can be written round the drawing or interspersed with it.

Depiction often seems to help us appreciate the symbolic nature of our re-presentations. It's easier to see that an object depicted in a drawing stands for more than the sum of its parts than words in a sentence. Perhaps drawings, because they are "holistic," can reflect tacit knowledge for us, where words, because they are linear, appear to demand explicitness.

One of my colleagues recently encouraged nine-year-olds to explore possibilities for stories they were going to write in groups, by first drawing their good and bad characters on large sheets of construction paper (divided from each other by a space in the middle); in the space they drew the place where these characters encountered each other. Key words were written around characters and meeting point, and arrows denoted movements back and forth.

Other children have "picture drafted" by cutting out their protagonists and moving them around on a picture map as they decided through collaborative talk how their story would take shape. Others have worked with a sequence of images on screen-folded paper—or on a "storyboard" with the page divided into squares.

Diagrams come into their own as an early form of reconstruction, especially where pupils have brainstormed for facts and need to find patterns for whatever information they have collected. Often children can collaborate to come up with highly inventive diagrams, which can then be used as helpful reference points for their subsequent investigations.

Clustering

I suppose clustering could be called a form of circular brainstorming. Instead of writing *down* the page, you write *round* the page, ringing a central key word with further ideas. Clustering can serve several functions in the exploratory stage of shaping meaning, and I will briefly define the functions that I have used with children, teenagers and adults.

Clustering can be used for both recollecting and reconstructing/recreating. I am indebted to Gabriele Lusser Rico's book *Writing the Natural Way* for providing so many interesting examples of how clustering can help the human brain to freewheel around a topic, allowing time for a fascinating variety of associations to emerge, amongst which, if the clusterer ponders, patterns may develop which can lead to new perceptions through free writing and drafting.

Using this strategy also reveals to students how diverse the personal meanings are that we can bring to a single word. No dictionary definition can ever capture the richness of associations that a cluster throws up, especially when these are shared by a whole group. The activity enables participants to discover how various the meanings can be that are attracted to the magnet word in the middle of the page—and how embedded in our own previous experiences.

In a somewhat similar way, in his book *Use Your Head* Tony Buzan recommends what he calls "patterning" as a useful exploratory strategy to rediscover what you know freed from the constraints of linear thinking. Buzan suggests that:

1. Words should be printed in capitals. For reading back purposes a printed pattern gives a more photographic, more immediate, and more comprehensive feedback.
2. The printed words should be on lines, and each line should be connected to other lines. This is to guarantee that the pattern has basic structure.
3. In creative efforts of this nature the mind should be left as "free" as possible. Any "thinking" about where things should go or whether they should be included will simply slow down the process. The idea is to recall everything your mind thinks of around the central idea.

The clusters in Figures 5–2 and 5–3 were made by a group of ten- to eleven-year-olds to re-present what they "now knew" about Australia after several weeks spent on researching that country. The children enjoyed constructing their clusters as a change from continuous writing; as a result of "patterning" what they knew, they were motivated to ask themselves further questions to find out more.

Where Rico encourages her students to draw rings round each thought so that their clusters look like bubbles or balloons, and Buzan encourages underlining, Donald Murray "maps" by loosely linking recollections as they occur to him with a series of dashes which indicate how one thought led to another. Though scattered across the page as they spread out from the topic word, Murray's thoughts in the example in Figure 5–4 already cluster roughly in "families" : food, past history, religion, relationships. A particular focus is then highlighted for further thinking by the arrows which draw together all the memories which feature religion from wherever they have cropped up on his freewheeling map.

As a way of drawing attention to the chameleon-like qualities of metaphor, clustering is also an excellent device as a form of wordplay which reveals how a whole network of expressions can grow from the root meaning of a single word (see Figure 5–5).

Several of the writing journeys that are given in full in the next chapter began from a clustering starting point. Being given the freedom to "spread out" their thoughts seems to appeal to older pupils as well as younger ones.

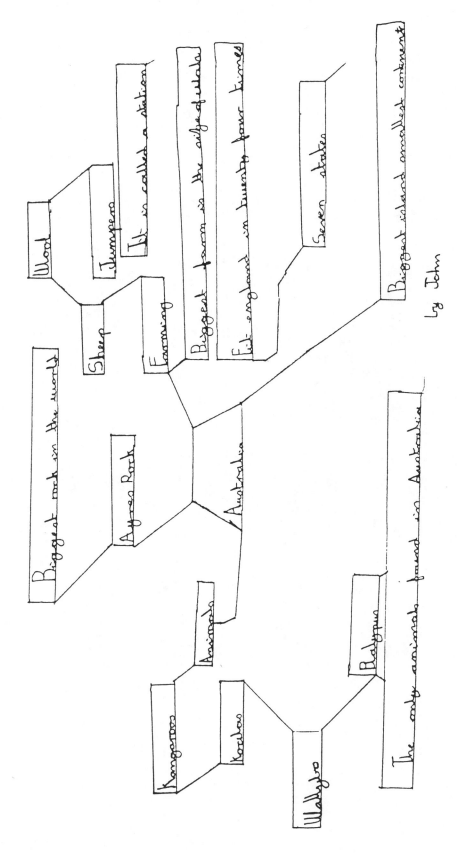

Figure 5–2 Chart on Australia

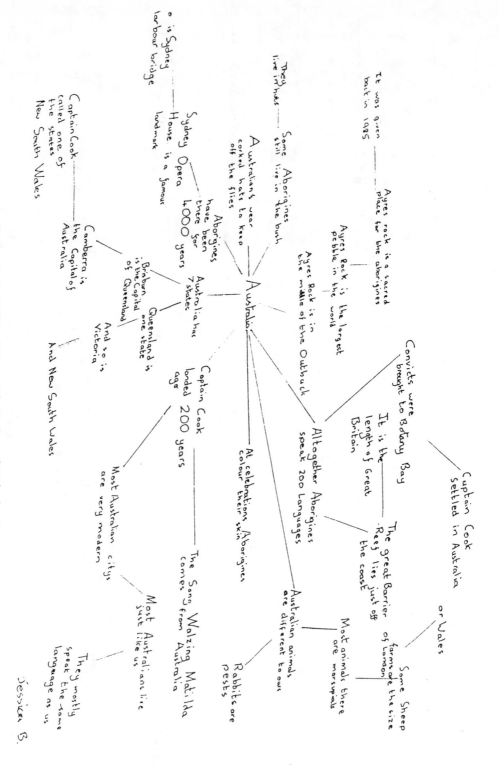

Figure 5-3 "What I Know About Australia" by Jessica

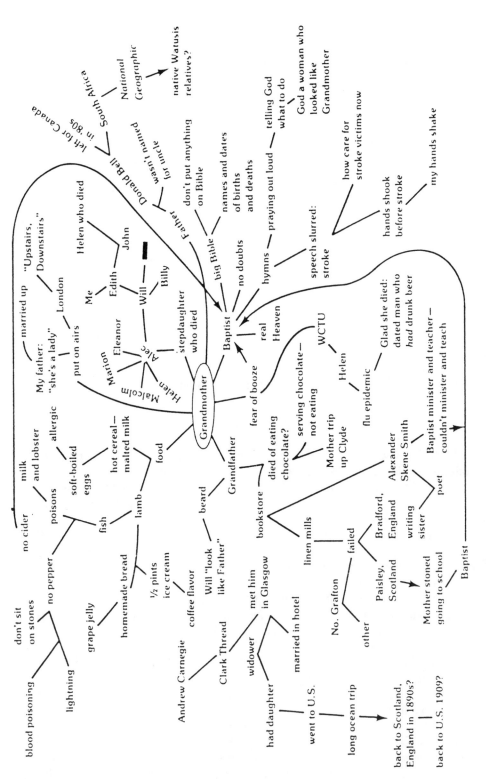

Figure 5–4 "Mapping" Cluster

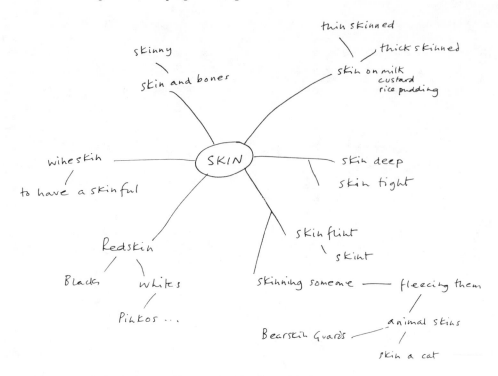

Figure 5–5 "Skin" Cluster

Free Writing

In some ways free writing is the simplest recollective starting point to offer to would-be writers but I have found that children launch into it more confidently if some of the other strategies I have just described have already convinced them that they really do have powerful computer-like brains that can respond to their requests.

Free writing can be focused or unfocused. I have already mentioned several examples of focused free writing—when the children are teleporting mentally for instance, or when they are thinking further about an item from a brainstormed list.

Not surprisingly, often what comes to mind when free writing is unfocused (i.e. left entirely to the writer without any initial suggestions), is a personal recollection such as the following:

My Nan—While she was sitting there I could of cried watching her sitting there with no motion She would speak but I knew if she was looking at me she wasn't speaking to me. Her left arm was dead it just laid there in her lap I could really cried and when we left the hospital I knew it could be the last time that I would ever see her and all I would have would be memories and photographs I walked out holding back the tears Suddenly I relized that she was not the only one I had to think about. My cousins liked us so much and wanted to come everywhere with us in the car on the way home David cried but not about Nan this time

Grandad who died in 1977 I did not no why he cried he was so close to Grandad but not uncle or nan. I had been close to my uncle, my sister too and the white mouse who lived in the cupboard or so he said The funeral was upsetting first the car and the man taking of his hat the service my sister crying Nan comforting her and the flowers and now Nan may be next very soon and all I will have will be memories of her sitting in the hospital all alone.

Or the writing may be a flight of fancy but based on real experience:

One day in a Pe lesson in the Summer 1989, we were throwing the motorised Javalin, these are Javelin with motors Which When thrown the Javelins motor starts going and helps the thrower to get more distance in his or her throw.

Our pe teacher demonstrated the way to throw these javels, he had one go And every dody around us were amazed it went throw straight up in the air and out of site then he said, "her it comes," I could see it landing 500-600 yards away. Then he asked if we wanted to use the new ones or the old, Well, I think you can guesse which one we chose.

We all went over to the throwing area and Picked up a motor Jav (motorised Javlin) and stood in a que getting ready, "Simon your first" said the teacher, I then walked back and started my run up, then I threw it, but a Failyer it only went about 10 Feet then I had another go, Christ it went miles compared to the first throw, it was about 300 yards

Or the writing may be a free think-write which is considering what will happen in the very real—and near, future:

What will I score on Saturday if so will it be a shot from about 30 yards or a powerful header. Will or will we score at all bet someone going to score because it a Cup match. Between Pottern social Club and I don't fancy going into extra time because I have only got little legs and iam the youngest because i play for a mens side. I expect a will be sub or not even play a might get hurt during the week playing rugby for example break my foot or my back might go again there wont be I wonder if we will have any hooligans and we they had to in the secound not play with any surporters Just think wound't that be funny if that happens to us. we might get banned from the league or the Cup. Just when I score a feeble goal or one of the other side scores in his own net and we win by that goal it would't be a very good Goal but a least we would get into the next round I would't care if all the goes were feeble but and we get into the final

I have given these examples of unfocused free writing because I think they illustrate how important it is for both students and teachers to recognize that this is a form of *exploratory thinking*.

So often kids who see themselves as rotten writers judge the quality of their writing—if they can grudgingly accept that it has any quality at all, by its length; and because very often it's like squeezing blood out of a stone, so do their teachers. The two lads, Mark and Derek, who produced the "motorized javelins" and the "will I score on Saturday" free writes were really pleased that as it turned out, they had written so many words in the space of ten minutes! At the age of fifteen, as "slow learners," they probably hadn't written so much which came directly from their own ideas for quite a long time. Nevertheless, I believe that we sell youngsters like this short if we accept, as a *draft*, ten- to fifteen-minutes worth of writing simply because it covers one side of paper.

I suppose if Derek and Mark had been encouraged to spend more time on their free writing, it would almost certainly have been as proofreaders. Although as yet there are only the seeds of possibilities in both pieces, the teacher would have regarded them as a draft that now needed editing—chiefly with regard to spelling and punctuation—and possibly some fairly minimal rewording. If on the other hand, she were to adopt a capacity-based approach which made it clear to these pupils that this initial writing was just a beginning, each of these free writings could have been used as the basis for further thinking/meaning shaping.

Finding a Focus

Response Partners Who Will Listen

Let's speculate for a paragraph or two about how Derek could have been helped to find a focus that would have given him a clearer sense of direction, when he came to spend rather longer than ten minutes, writing a draft about his hopes for the Saturday match. Derek could have found a partner to read his free write aloud to. Hearing his own words come off the page can in itself give a writer further ideas. But it helps to have a friendly audience who will also *listen* to what the writer has to say about the thoughts and feelings that he has recollected so far. I find after participating in many writing workshops, that it is more helpful initially, for the writer to use a partner as a receptive *listener*, not as an instant *responder*. Responding immediately to someone else's writing, even at this exploratory stage, is not easy—for children or indeed for adults. It either leads to rather vague commendatory comments or to nit-picking.

On the other hand, if the writer is given a chance to expand and possibly to clarify for his own benefit as well as for his partner's what this free write has put into (or pulled out of?) his mind, he will then be in a better position to set off again, because in a sense, he has now looked ahead. If I were the teacher, I would not encourage comment on specific words and phrases; that is more appropriate for the next pause for breath once the first draft has been completed. At this "viewing point," I would rather encourage a much broader discussion of the writer's intentions as a meaning-shaper, into which the partner who has listened may be drawn—but in response to what the writer thinks and feels, not as a critic of his words on page or screen.

I can only speculate about what Derek might have said to his partner, but my guess is that he would have said more about his team, their strengths and weaknesses—and more about his feelings: being the youngest on the team, perhaps not even getting a chance to play at all—and how great it would be if he really did score that winning goal! Without any further suggestions, just with this chance to reflect on what he has recollected so far, I believe that Derek could have then produced a more coherent, extended draft.

Asking Open Questions

Where the teacher is acting as responder, at this juncture between the exploratory stage and the draft, her job also is not yet to look *at* the words but to look *through* them to the emerging meanings on which the writer may wish to focus, and after she has listened, to ask him a few questions for further consideration. If I had been responding to Derek in this way, I might have asked:

> Will you be very disappointed if your team loses? How long have you been playing for them? How come you got in the side so young? Do you often have hooligans at matches? Any suggestions about how to deal with them? Does your team really have a chance of getting through to the final?

These are all meaning-related questions to encourage some first draft extended writing, with their "tell me more" kind of invitation. But there are also questions which can focus the writer's attention on the form he would like his first draft to take:

> What's going to be the best way of writing this in draft? As a letter to a mate of yours who won't laugh at your hopes and fears? Two letters perhaps, one before the match and one after? Or that "determination to win," could you concentrate those feelings into a short poem—or write a story about a team who ruined their chances because they were determined to win *at any cost.* You could write from the viewpoint of being the youngest—or of having a friend who's got mixed up with a bunch of football hooligans. Read your free write through again and decide what you most want to focus on in your draft. Leave everything else out.

If you are helping another writer to find a sense of direction before moving on to a continuous draft, it's important to make it clear that you are only offering suggestions and that the writer is not bound to follow any of them. If she rejects them all, at least having decided what she doesn't want to do, she is in a better position to decide what she does! I am sure however that suggestions *at this point* in the writing journey are more likely to be helpful to the writer than a comment at the end. In responding to work in progress at this early stage, there are still many options open to both writer and responder. At the very least, the teacher is helping the student to find out what kind of questions she can fruitfully ask herself. One of our problems as teachers is that if we can find no time at all to write ourselves, it is difficult to know what questions could be helpful to other writers. Perhaps that is why for so long we have tended to stick to being conscientious proofreaders and minimal responders to meaning.

In *Write to Learn* Murray suggests eighteen different ways in which those first recollections can be " circled" by the writer in the search for perspectives that will take him into a continuous draft. I find that for schoolchildren a few of these directional questions are helpful, but they get overfaced if they are offered too many. But it's early days yet—if a capacity-based approach were to be offered to all learners throughout their school years, who knows what advances in writerly techniques would become possible.

Drafting

For me, drafting is a useful word for referring to that stage of the writing journey which the writer needs to undertake alone—and usually for a longer stretch than any of the exploratory excursions that I have just described. This is the stage at which the writer knows where she is heading—and sets out. The most sustained meaning-making happens now, as the brain sets to work on probing further the possibilities that have most attracted the writer about the thoughts, images, feelings which have shown up in those early explorations. At this stage the writer needs to be able to settle down without distractions, attending only to the renewed process of discovery that is taking place inside her own head. As the words come into earshot and are made visible through her fingertips, they will draw towards them the next utterance and then the next. If she keeps going the draft will unroll, maybe not in one sitting, but often more speedily than many students imagine—if only they will concentrate on becoming attentive listeners to their own thoughts taking shape.

As far as possible I try to encourage students when they are drafting, to keep their mental eyes and ears just on the step ahead, so that they keep moving forward steadily. They need to know that there will be time to have a closer look at the landscape later—once they have brought it into being. So, still no immediate concern with mechanics or with the minutiae of meaning but rather with the flow, and seeing where it takes them. There has to be a strong impulse to push forward in producing that first continuous draft, which overrides minor difficulties—and *never* stops for whiteout!

The Editing Stage

Editing for Meaning

Traditionally (by which I mean until very recently in some schools and commonly still in most), writing is regarded as a one-off activity by most pupils. They are given a writing task—to produce a story or a description or an account of a book they have read or a project—and they simply go ahead and write it, sometimes in school time and sometimes for homework. If they are secondary age, they then hand in what they have written (without additional help or consultation during the writing time), for the teacher to grade. This usually involves marking for omitted or incorrect surface features along with a brief comment on the "quality" of the writing as the teacher perceives it. Comments such as "Remember paragraphs" and "Not a bad effort but next time try to improve your style" are fairly typical. Sometimes of course the teacher's observations are more perceptive than this but it is still rare for most pupils to rework what they have written once the teacher has given the grade.

Thanks to the work of the National Writing Projects for the last decade in the USA and for the past three years in the UK, along with the now widely disseminated writings of researchers such as Donald Graves and his team, this one-off approach to writing is changing. Most recently the UK Examining Boards for the new General Certificate of Secondary Education (GCSE) at 16 + have acknowledged the value of drafts which can now be submitted alongside finished pieces of work in pupils' folders as additional evidence of the writer's thoughtful application to the task.

How the drafting process is defined, is still open to a variety of inter-pretations. Does the exploratory short burst writing that I have described in some detail in this chapter constitute a draft? And is there a recognizable point at which a first draft becomes a second—or a third? I am not really concerned to tighten up on these definitions; better that drafting is left open to individuals to interpret according to context and as it works best for them.

What I *do* think important is the recognition that if writing is about meaning-shaping, it is essential that opportunities are made available *for further reflection*—to extend and to clarify our initial attempts at formulation. The "model" that I have outlined in this chapter offers such opportunities specifically *before* a continuous draft is embarked upon and *after* that first draft has been completed. In the first instance the pupil has some exploratory writing and possibly drawing to consider as she seeks to find a focus and a form that will take her further; in the second instance she has made a sustained excursion which she can now sit back and mull over at a more leisurely pace.

Changes can be made to a first draft in a variety of ways. If the writer is using a word processor as I am, she may make multiple changes as she moves backward and forward over the ground already covered. There will be no definable second or third draft—just a continual reworking of the original, possibly on two or three separate occasions, until the writer is satisfied with what it says and how it sounds. In this respect, perhaps it makes more sense to think in terms of two or three different "visits" to the initial draft rather than two or three separate drafts.

On paper it is easier to track and to preserve a history of the changes that are made than on the word processor, as the writer crosses out or pencils in alternative versions, sometimes in a small way—sometimes at length. Or the writer may choose to rewrite a complete second version with her first draft alongside for reference—or to use Berthoff's double-entry notebook technique, with space to make any lengthy emendations on the page opposite the original draft.

What matters is that at the post-first-draft stage, the writer is encouraged to edit for *meaning* first, before paying attention to the task of proofreading. In my experience, too many teachers still regard any editing as primarily a matter of correction. Yet if pupils are encouraged to think carefully about the meaning of what they have written and to make changes where appropriate, their finished product is often strikingly improved. At this point in their meaning-shaping journey I am finding that young writers will now cut out and condense—as well as extend a point here and there, as they listen again to their own first thoughts and get their "ear in" to the rhythms that already reside in the words on the page. They can often hear these more clearly on a rereading, when their attention is no longer focused on the step ahead.

Teachers often say to me that if their pupils are given the impression that every piece of writing will need to be rewritten over and over again, then surely their attitude to writing will deteriorate even further! My response is to emphasize that first and foremost we need to convince our pupils that writing is an exciting *act of discovery* and that secondly it offers each of them an excellent opportunity to shape their own meanings. Sometimes this shaping will come easily and sometimes it will be difficult but if they are offered the kind of strategies for making the journey that are outlined here, the compulsion to get the whole thing over and done with as quickly as possible soon disappears. I hope that the examples of pupil writing which come into the next chapter will give some indication of how teachers can help that change of emphasis to take place.

Editing for Correctness

Proofreading comes last of all, before a fair copy is made for publication to a wider audience; at this final stage, mechanics deserve the close and concentrated attention of the writer. It is at this point, nearing journey's end and with the sense of ownership and satisfaction that comes from "making it," that the teacher can helpfully point out any common misspelling patterns (such as doubled letters, omitted letters, and reversals) with a real chance that the writer will listen and take note. Encourage pupils to proofread for each other; if their attention is drawn to helping a friend spot spelling errors and punctuation omissions, this will also raise their own awareness of correct encoding. For far too long teachers have taken it upon themselves alone to act as conscientious, some would say obsessive, proofreaders—often when the writers were not even present!

To recap—however smoothly or effortfully a writing journey is made, basically three stages of meaning-shaping are involved: an exploratory stage which may involve several modes of expression—especially brief "bursts" of writing, talking, drawing, mapping, diagramming; a continuous draft; and the revision or editing of that draft for meaning and for mechanics.

Re-presentation

Once the meaning-shaping is complete, the writer can then choose how she wants her work to be presented. I feel strongly that any writing which has achieved the status of a finished product in the eyes of the pupil and the teacher, should be given the opportunity for presentation to a wider audience, either within the student's own peer group or beyond that.

A journey that has been successfully completed deserves to be shared with others—and shared in the way that all published writing is shared, in a magazine collection, as a leaflet or booklet, as an artistic artifact: a poem sheet or a hardback book or whatever. In my own county, children from the ages of five to sixteen have learned how to make their own unique and beautiful books, which can then be shared—with their permission, with other readers. I know that this move into carefully crafted bookmaking is now far more widespread—in secondary as well as primary schools, and I welcome it with much enthusiasm. It is an excellent way of motivating young writers from the start, to take their meaning-shaping seriously and to sustain it to the point where the finished story, poetry anthology or information booklet can be proudly handled by the authors *and* by their readers. I have to say that I would like to see more excellent GCSE finished pieces which have accomplished a complete writing journey, being celebrated with a wider audience also—as well as receiving the required embalmment in folders for examiners to scrutinize.

6

Shaping Meaning

Moving Towards
a Finished Product

Some Real Writing Journeys

In the previous chapter I described the three broad stages for shaping meaning that pupils of all ages can be offered, whether they are reception infants or GCSE students. This chapter offers the evidence—examples of how children in primary and secondary schools have responded to the opportunities which their teachers have provided to explore, to draft, and to edit—or in capacity-based terms, to recollect, to re-create or reconstruct, and finally, to re-present.

Conkers

These six-year-olds had been doing a project on trees. When one of the Wiltshire Writing Project team visited the school, she asked the children to choose a favorite tree and in pairs to recollect whatever came into their minds when they thought about that tree. As Figure 6–1 shows, Camilla and Valerie chose a horse chestnut tree and wrote:

conker fell out of Its caes and landed on some yellow levs and the caes is very prickaley the conker is brown the caes of the conker is brown as well. conker is very shinee the conker is very smooth on the top and on the bottom it is rugth and white the conker tree is desidyous as the coler of the borc is brown the conker tree flows in summer and the branhis have little buds onit You can put conkers on string You can have conkers fites and swing them about.

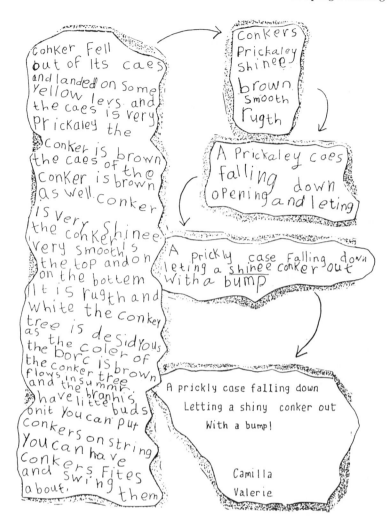

Figure 6–1   Conkers

I don't know whether Camilla and Valerie took turns writing down these details about "the conker tree"—the firm clear printing in which their knowledge was written down looked as though it had been formed by the same hand throughout. What is lost of course, by its very nature is the collaborative chatter that accompanied the writing. We cannot now tell to what extent the concentration of the two little girls was sustained by their shared talk, although the variety of recalled details suggests that working in twos was a help not a hindrance.

They were then asked to choose six key words out of what they had written, which captured whatever was most important to them about their tree. They selected: *conkers, prickaley, shinee, brown, smooth, rugth.*

Jo, their teacher, then talked about word-pictures to the class and about how we can all see pictures in our minds. She also read aloud several haiku before inviting the children to return to their lists and have a go at making their own word-picture poem. Camilla and Valerie began by writing:

A prickaley caes falling down opening and leting

They then stopped in mid-sentence, had another think and wrote:

> **A prickly case falling down**
> **Leting a *shinee* conker out**
> **With a bump**

Their teacher then proofread their poem with them so that the final jumbo typed version included an extra "t" in letting and replaced the double "ee" with a "y" in shiny. An exclamation mark completed the final line.

Of course the poem shape that this writing took was strongly influenced by Jo's suggestions—as was the "writing to find out what you know" which preceded the poem. The children could just as well have been asked to draw first and then to write down some key words to go with their drawing. So much of what children do in school depends upon what their teacher does and how their teacher thinks!

On this occasion, these children had the chance to pick up on the following important notions about writing in this small sequence of activities: that writing can help you to find out what you know—and can make what you know visible to other people; that writing can include the thoughts of more than one person; that writing can *change its shape* and that writing as a code, can be corrected.

The Crystal Planet

This next writing journey for infants grew out of a couple of drama sessions in which everybody spent time first of all preparing for their flight, and secondly exploring their own planets once they had arrived on them. Looked at from a writing perspective, these sessions and the imaginative thinking and talking they involved, form an important part of the exploratory stage of the writing journey that grew from them—as does the picture map of their planet which the children drew next. Looked at from the broader perspective of shaping meaning, each activity possesses its own validity, which doesn't have to lead anywhere other than towards its own power to shape. As the earlier chapters of this book suggest, our mental capacities for shaping meaning continually interrelate, making use of whatever media happen to be at hand—verbal, visual or kinetic. Thus written words can just as easily become part of the exploratory stage of an art or a music or even a maths journey as the other way round. Because this book takes writing as its central focus, my examples show written language becoming the dominant mode of expression. In the overall context of learning across the whole curriculum, other expressive modes may equally well become dominant. Writing doesn't *always* have to be the concluding activity!

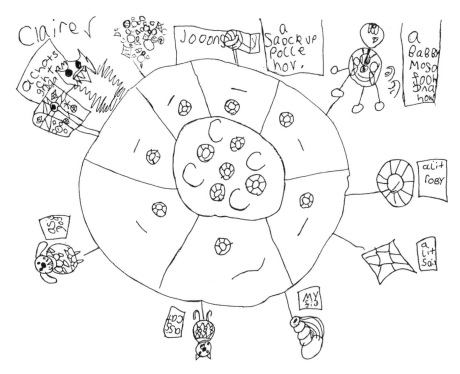

Figure 6–2   Claire's Picture Map

To return to six-year-old Claire—the picture map that she drew of her planet is shown in Figure 6–2.

When translated, the words that she wrote around the edges in her emergent, early phonic writing, read (moving clockwise from 12:00): jewels, a suck-up Hoover, a baby monster fallen down a hole, a little ruby, a little star, my (?), a space cat, a space dog and a treasure chest guarded by a monster. Claire called her planet the Crystal Planet.

Next in her own writing she expanded these "key" words in Figure 6–3, along with a further drawing of herself in her spaceship which looks remarkably like a suck-up Hoover itself! The translation is as follows:

> When we landed we saw a monster guarding some treasure and a pile of jewels [. . . diamonds] and a suck-up Hoover. A monster [child?] and a space cat and a space dog.

I think the other words on the left read, "I made a friend out of monster" but I'm not sure—especially in the light of what happens in Claire's final draft!

Claire's teacher encouraged her to continue her writing journey for longer than she would probably have managed without any companion. She talked with her about her map, her words and her picture. Before she embarked on her final version, Claire confided that she was going to con-

Figure 6–3   Claire's Expanded Story

centrate on the monster and leave out the other creatures on her list. It was that sort of shared enterprise.

The translation of her final version (see Figure 6–4) is as follows:

We were flying to space and then we ran out of fuel! We had to land. We saw blue sparkling jewels. The planet was sticky. We saw a monster guarding some treasure. We waited until the monster was asleep then we [?] in and the monster woke up and it chased us and we ran to [?]. Then we killed it and the treasure was ours and we were rich.

Shaping Meaning from a Science Experiment

In many respects, this sequence of writing from James, who is seven years old, could equally well have been included in the next chapter which focuses on pupils writing to "make sense." I chose to include it here, because James's account of what he did and what he thought, moves through two of his own drafts and a final version scribed for him by his teacher. He is clarifying and extending his explanation (with the help of his teacher), in order to achieve a finished piece of writing which can be displayed to their joint satisfaction for a wider audience.

It is much easier to recognize a literary finished product which takes

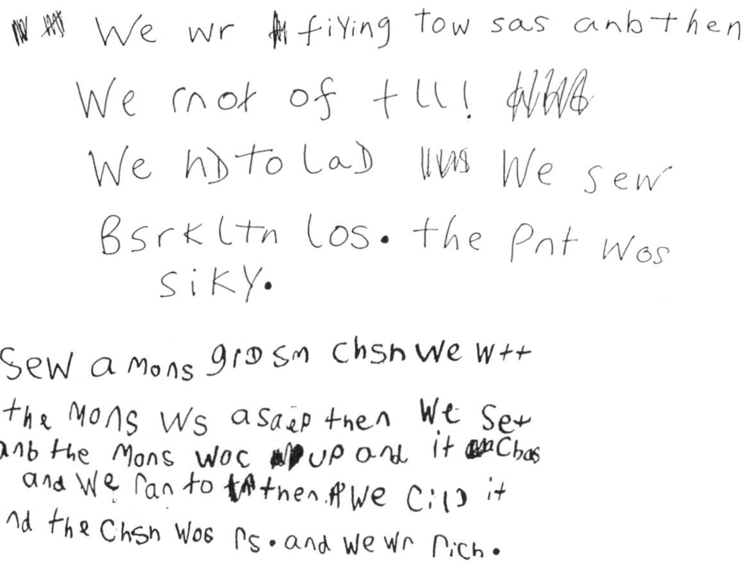

We wr fiying tow sas anb then
We mot of tll! We hD to LaD We sew
Bsrk Ltn Los. the Pnt was siky.

We sew a mons grD sm chsh we wtt
intll the Mons Ws asaep then Wt Sey
in anb the Mons woc up and it Chas
as and We ran to th then We Cilp it
and the Chsh Wos rs. and we wr rich.

Figure 6–4   Claire's Final Version

the familiar shape of a story or a poem, than one which is "nonliterary." In adult writing, nonfiction can take the form of an article or a paper, an essay or a textbook. We do not expect children of James's age to produce any such finished products; nevertheless, in the sequence shown in Figure 6–5, the writer develops both his grasp of the code of written language and the meaning which he seeks to convey through it, as he moves from first to second draft, and finally with oral elaboration, to his "last say" on the subject.

Sally Logs Her Own Writing Journeys

The next example also comes from a class of seven- to eight-year-olds in a small village school. Their teacher asked them to keep a record of a complete writing journey, along with their own thoughts at each stage of that journey, by sticking their progressive stages and comments on each stage into a large stapled-together construction-paper book.

To start with all the children clustered their own ideas in single words and phrases around the magnet word COLD. Sally's cluster appears in Figure 6–6. Sally then wrote underneath this on a separate piece of paper:

First we did a brainstorm on cold on our own. We shared with another person got more words down and then we shared with another person. I thought the brainstorm was going to be hard but it wasn't because once we got started I found I knew lots of words.

Sally then drew the picture diagram shown in Figure 6–7 which included a tree with bare branches, a house with icicles hanging from it, a sheet of

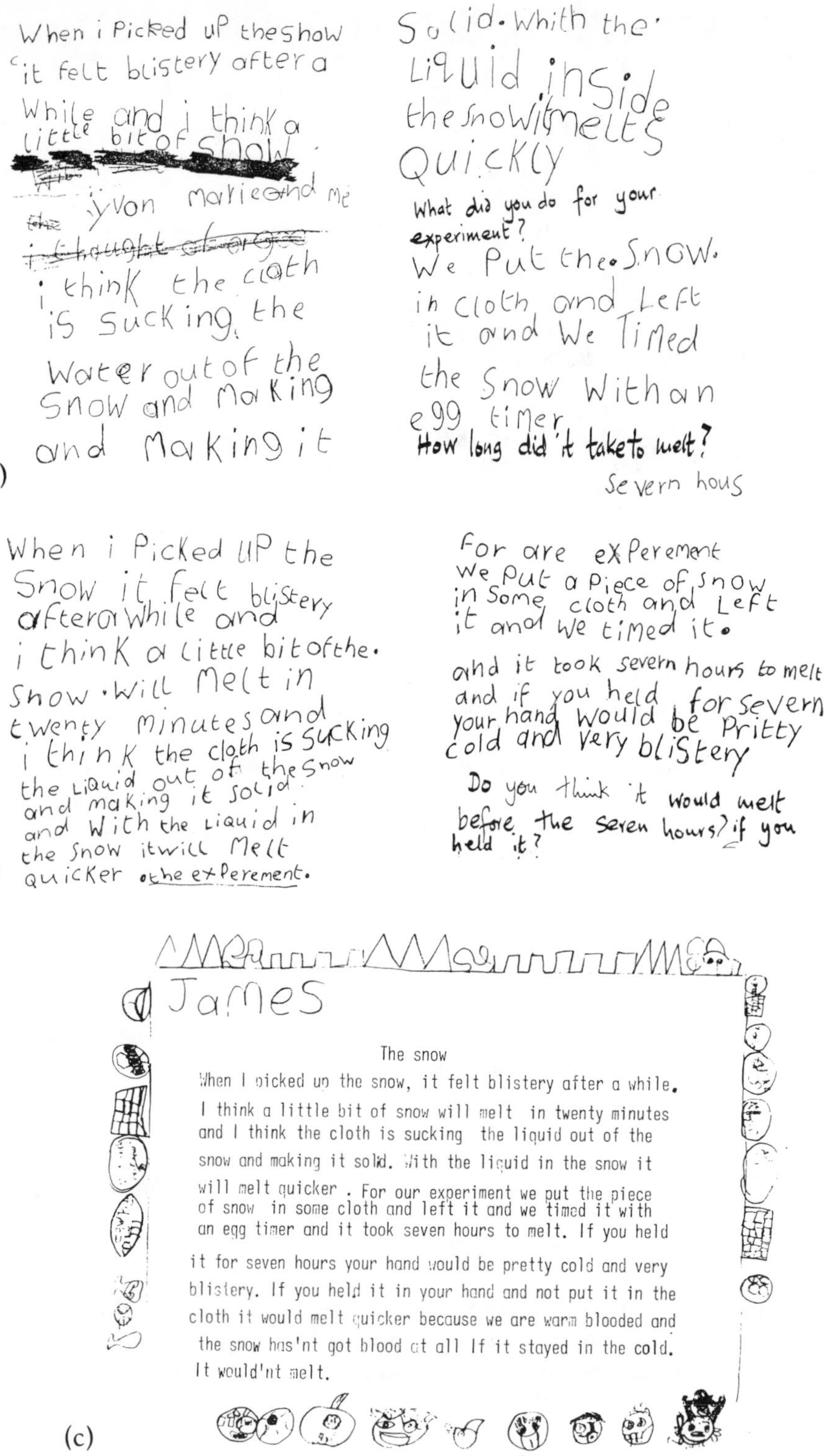

(a)

When i picked up the show
it felt blistery after a
while and i think a
little bit of snow.
yvon marrie and me
i thought of a
i think the cloth
is sucking the
water out of the
snow and making
and making it

Solid. whith the
liquid inside
the snow it melts
quickly

What did you do for your
experiment?
We put the snow
in cloth and left
it and we timed
the snow with an
egg timer.
How long did it take to melt?

Severn hous

(b)

When i picked up the
Snow it felt blistery
after a while and
i think a little bit of the.
Snow. will melt in
twenty minutes and
i think the cloth is sucking
the liquid out of the snow
and making it solid.
and with the liquid in
the snow it will melt
quicker. the experement.

For are experement
we put a piece of snow
in some cloth and left
it and we timed it.

and it took severn hours to melt
and if you held
your hand would be for severn
cold and very blistery

Do you think it would melt
before the seven hours? if you
held it?

(c)

James

The snow

When I picked up the snow, it felt blistery after a while.

I think a little bit of snow will melt in twenty minutes
and I think the cloth is sucking the liquid out of the
snow and making it solid. With the liquid in the snow it

will melt quicker. For our experiment we put the piece
of snow in some cloth and left it and we timed it with
an egg timer and it took seven hours to melt. If you held

it for seven hours your hand would be pretty cold and very
blistery. If you held it in your hand and not put it in the
cloth it would melt quicker because we are warm blooded and
the snow has'nt got blood at all If it stayed in the cold.
It would'nt melt.

Figure 6–5   James's Work   (a) First Draft   (b) Second Draft
(c) Final Version

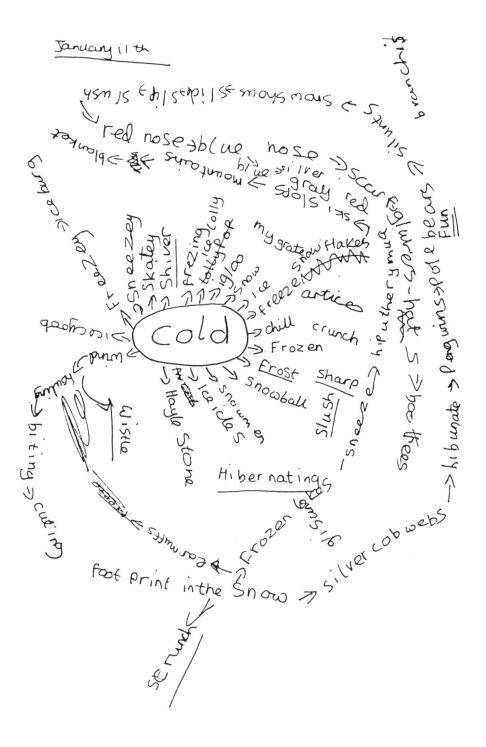

Figure 6–6   Sally's "Cold" Cluster

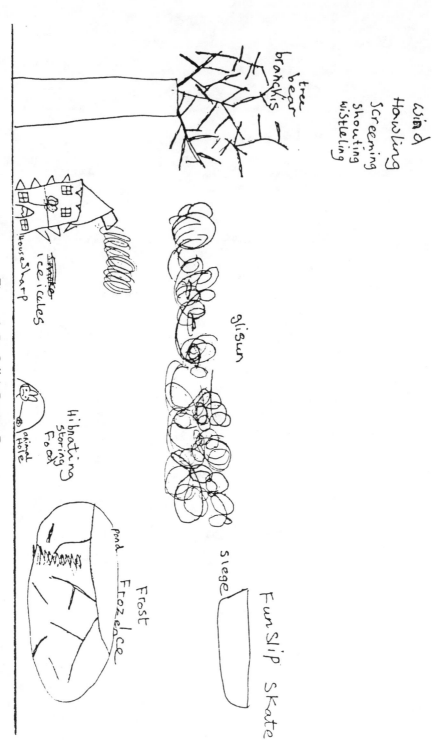

Figure 6–7 Sally's Picture Diagram

glistening ice, a frozen pond with the ice cracking on it, a *slege* and a rabbit in a hole. Underneath she wrote:

Then I drew a picture. It made you think, you could make your words up together. It helped me choose what words I wanted to use.

Next Sally produced a short piece of what she refers to underneath as "burst writing":

1 day it was very cold and I got my scarf and hat and gluves on and my coat and went out to play I walked by the pound it had ice all over it then I looked at the tree it was bear and branches were hanging off. The wind was howling wistleling and screming.
burst writing helped me start my poem because there were rhymy bits in it. Burst writing was very helpful but for then I did'nt think I could do it with out stopping but I did do it.

When Sally came to write what she calls her first draft, she had decided on a poem:

> **out side the snow was falling**
> **the icicles are hanging**
> **The Pound was Frosun**
> **the trees were bear**
> **the wind was howling screaming**
> **the animals hibernating ready for the winter**
> **The slege all iced up**
> **Footsteps crunch through the crustey snow**

Sally's comment on her draft reads:

First I read the poem out to every body then Mrs F told me to read it out without the thes and I thought it was much better. Then she said to try and re-arrange the words and to take some of the ings away and I thought it was much better as well. you have to take a lot of words out when you write a poem.

Sally's next set of comments read:

Then I got my spellings checked. Then I started my neat copy. After that I read it to my self and I thought it sounded very good I felt very proud of myself I liked it very much. The best bit I liked was when it said Footsteps crunch through the snow.

Sally's fair copy is shown in Figure 6–8—it completes her "Writing Journey."
Sally was so taken with these strategies for shaping meaning that she went home and undertook every stage of that same journey with splendid confidence entirely on her own! Next day she came into school with a four-page homemade book into which she had glued her "Island" brainstorm,

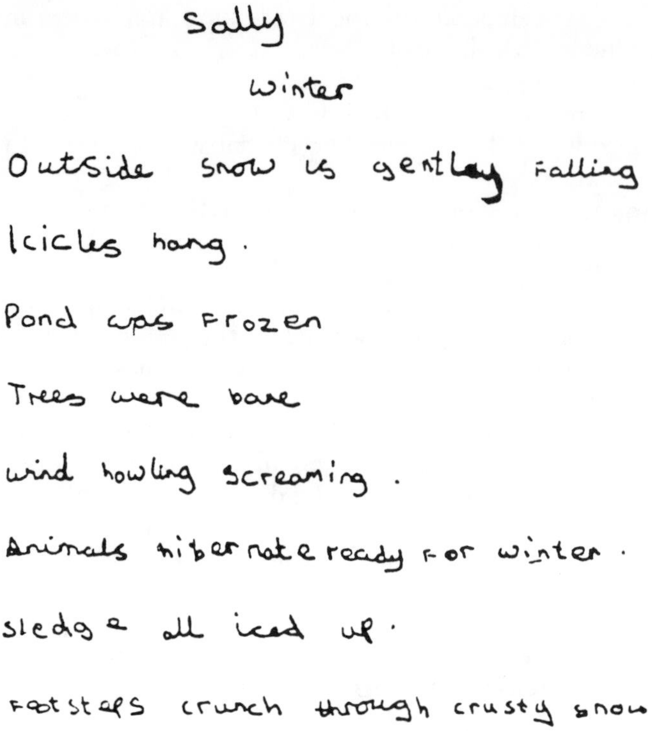

Sally

winter

Outside snow is gently falling

Icicles hang.

Pond was frozen

Trees were bare

wind howling screaming.

Animals hibernate ready for winter.

sledge all iced up.

Footsteps crunch through crusty snow

Figure 6–8   Sally's Fair Copy

her comment on it ("brain storming is easy at school but not at home because you can share with other people at school but you cant at home [but] if you know how to do it at school you can do it at home like I can") her burst writing, her draft and her fair copy, which is a story encapsulating Good winning over Evil on her desert island in the space of fifteen lines—a major effort for a nearly eight-year-old!

Searching for a Subject-and Eventually Finding It!

At nearly eight Sally is already well on the way to being a competent encoder as well as a confident and enthusiastic writer. At ten, in a top junior class, Jessica is often incomprehensible still to another reader—so much so on occasions, that it would be easy to make the mistake that we are so often prone to do if we rely on the simplistic observation of surface features, that Jessica has few ideas because her writing literally tends to screw them up. Nothing could be further from the truth. In the second half of the spring term in this class, Jessica along with everyone else had been jotting down some short bursts of writing as a way of discovering what she most wanted to write about. She records in her writing diary:

To day I writo Done three Sucks. 1. boy 2. Brid 3. romance I thaink that Brid came frst nest romance then Boys.

In fact none of these short bursts had been at all productive. Several children in the class had decided to write about old age however, and two weeks later in her writing diary Jessica records:

old people
Im geting on well ckwte selly I think it myt be chit nos I think of bag
My wrigth was good I mad a slit call of my end of my wrigth.

A week later comes the entry:

I hav finchd wiring it in rufe I think It Qiyt good

and the next day:

I am coping cawt.

And on the next day:

Ive fenigd the writing I think Mr Brown like it I am plest wiht it.

Figure 6–9 is a photocopy of Jessica's revised first draft, along with her own fair copy. The underlined words in the draft are where she asked for help; her teacher mostly wrote the correct spellings over the top of her original version as it would have been too laborious for her to rub out and rewrite every misspelling.

Who would have thought, least of all Jessica perhaps, that such a strong and tender piece of writing would emerge from her initial fumblings—and look at the tremendous improvement too in her handwriting for that fair copy. She is justifiably proud of what she has written and willing to make a considerable investment of time and effort for her finished piece. Her work provides the strongest of arguments for continuing to tap sources of genuine concern in all children. Such a piece could never have emerged from a textbook exercise "designed" to improve Jessica's "encoding skills"—and yet so many pupils with similar difficulties are constrained to spend withdrawal time "exercising"—with no attention paid to how locating their own concerns can empower them to shape meaning and *to discover how to write* at the same time.

Death of a Cat

I have chosen my final example of a primary-age child's writing journey, because it is also a drawing journey with a rough sketch that precedes the finished picture, in just the way the early writing precedes the computer printout. (See Figure 6–10.)

The class (top juniors) had been asked to brainstorm individually for memories that brought back strong feelings (1). Joanne then chose the death of her cat as the memory that she wanted to re-create (2). The rest

(a)   Jessica

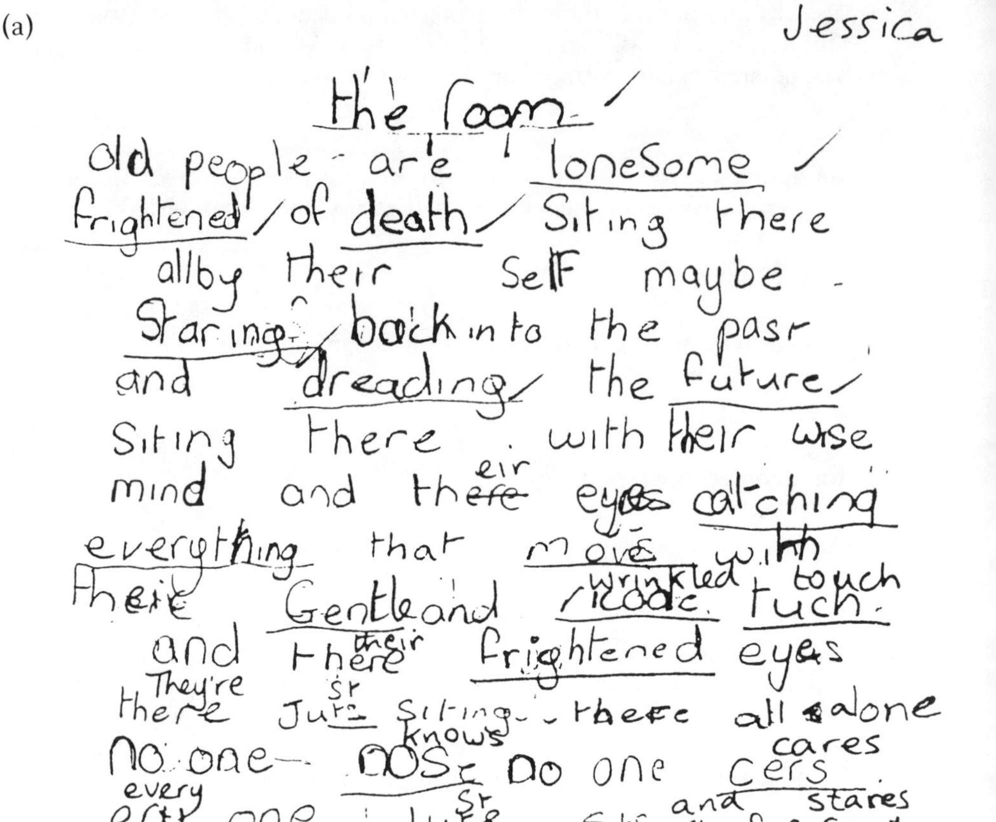

the room /
old people are lonesome /
frightened / of death / Siting there
allby their self maybe .
Staring / back into the past
and dreading / the future /
Siting there . with their wise
mind and theeir eyes catching
everything that move with
their Gentle and wrinkled tuch .
and their frightened eyes
They're
there just siting . there all alone
knows   cares
no one— nose no one cers .
every   and stares
ery one just sits a sered
and oldness gros grows
knows
and no one they sit a bne
moan
and they mone
suddenly
death   and suduley
deth has is Calling falling
and falling
knows   person goes
noone naws when this pursun gost
Shes . Just lying there
under   earth   under
unber the erehln and unber the
ruth turf.

Figure 6-9 Jessica's Work (a) Revised First Draft (b) Final Fair Copy

(b)

The room

Old people are lonesome
Frightened of death Siting there
allby their self may be
Staring back in at the past
and dreding the future
Siting there with their wise
mind and their eyes catching
everything that moves with
their Gentlu and wrinkld touch
and their frightened eyes
Theyre Jusr Siting there all alone
noone knows noone cares
every one Jusr sits and stairs
and oldness grows and noone knows
they sit alone and they moan
and Suddenly
death is calling
noone knows when this person goes
she Jusr lying there
under the earth and under the
turf.

The End

Jessica

10yrs.

(Sad) Cat died Poly

(sad) Sat next to my greatgran holding her hand
When she died

riding my bike down hill rolled into a
lampost

fire in some fields.

fell off slide play school

I was with my parents and sister.'
at home I was in the hall
I stood still and dropped the shopping
bags then started to cry.

1

What I Saw

Came through open front door
into hall

dad came out of living room and told
me.

dark room

Sad faces
Stiff cat

What I felt

I felt happy when I came through front door
everything fell upside down
weard
when I heard I stood stiff just
like the cat
I walked into the living room
Just as I walked my heart began to
hurt
nelt down and
started to cry.
after I felt nothing.

2

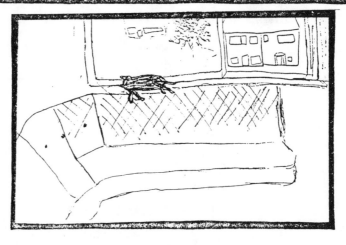

Figure 6–10   Joanne's Work

I stood still just like the cat.

  I started walking ,

As I walked my heart began to hurt.

Then I knelt down and started to cry.

    After .....I felt nothing.

    Joanne

Figure 6–10   continued

is self-explanatory, especially as the drawings and the words complement each other.

Footsteps Haiku

Two years older than Joanne, Stephen has similarly intermingled writing and drawing in an exploration which moves from a cluster through several drafts which include sketches as well as words to a final haiku that is both visual and verbal (see Figure 6–11).

I include Stephen's poem as well as Joanne's partly because I like them both, but also just to make the point briefly that it is impossible to take the variable of age to measure the "progress" of one child against another. The fact that Stephen is in a 2nd-year secondary class and Joanne in the top juniors doesn't mean that *for that reason* we should expect the boy to produce a poem of higher quality than the girl. What produces quality as we glimpsed so powerfully with Jessica's poem, is the depth of feeling that inspires the writer as she dwells on those inward searchings to encapsulate. Finished pieces from these children are not included in order to be compared, but to be enjoyed for what they are and for what the children have succeeded in shaping often from hesitant beginnings.

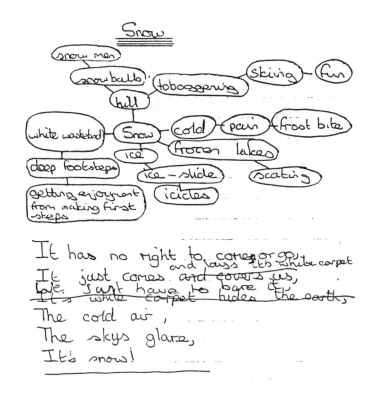

(a)

Figure 6–11   Stephen's Work   (a) Cluster and Draft   (b) More Drafts and Final
Haiku

It falls, white, covering everything,
Everything stops, its taken control,
Snow is here.
                    is only
everything stops,
snow has it's hold . . . but only
until tommorow.

It falls, white, covering everything,
everybody stops,
Snow has it's hold...But only until Sunday.

Haiku

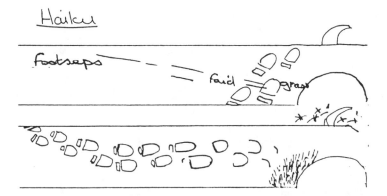

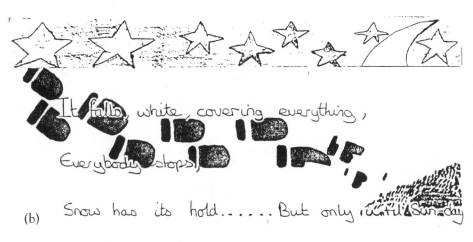

It falls, white, covering everything,
Everybody stops,
(b)   Snow has its hold......But only until Sunday

by Stephen   2J

Monsters

No English program would be complete without the theme of Monsters cropping up with a fair amount of regularity! This 1st-year secondary group had read several poems together from the Lobel/Prelutsky *Nightmares* collection as well as the Grendel episode from the Beowulf Saga. They then all drew their monsters with the aim of frightening little children! Stuart's first sketches are shown in Figure 6–12.

They then talked about their drawings with a partner and asked each other questions like "Where does it live?" "What are its habits?" "Tell me more about its appearance." Here are some of the further details that Stuart jotted down after this discussion:

hairy, skin bumpy, fingers Monsterouis, eyes scary, pi(m)ply, spotty, ugly, Mad, stupied, bogaly eyes.
big headed, fungious face, boggle eyed, gross eyed, slavering Jaws (crossed out)

Tairs out children's brains, pulls their body in half, pulls off their toes one by one, chopps up there eyes into slic(e)s
He moves through people grave digging under ground
Under the bed, behind the cuboard, lurks in the graveyard
On a misty night he appears at 12 midnight
his claws make good spad(e)s
claws make good spades.

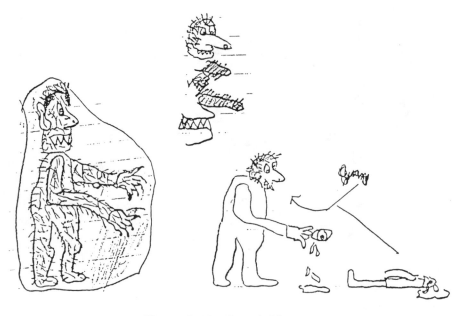

Figure 6–12   Stuart's Monsters

Stuart then brainstormed his own list of "good words" he might use. I quote it horizontally rather than vertically to save space:

shadow, shawdow, greatness, bloody gora (?) deadly sharp, sharpness, hidous head, greasly mouth, steaming smoke, trickelying blood, grasp, snalded (?) horrow, ferce, sucles his blood

It is evident that Stuart is not short of ideas and indeed is tackling his subject with the sort of relish that monster-creation often induces amongst the young! In view of this sense of commitment to his task, his first draft is perhaps somewhat disappointing:

> **On one deep and misty night at 12 midnight**
> **I was walking past the graveyard,**
> **On my way home, and I noticed something**
> **Out-rageous**
> **It was a hairy thing?**
> **I could not**
> **Make out.**
> **I decided to go closer, and to my**
> **Suprise! I saw a hariy monster!**
> **It was lurking in the mist, trying to**
> **Find something to eat.**
> **It saw me, I started to run, "so did**
> **He", he was gaining on me.**
> **He caught me up and grabbed me**
> **By the neck.**
> **He crushed my bones and sucked my**
> **Blood and ground me to a pulp**
> **I was no more, but he was still**
> **Living.**

Stuart's second version recounts this event in the third person and after the first four lines reverts to prose:

Midnight in a misty graveyard
A grewsome thing was lurking.
Just waiting for his pray.
A small boy was runing
The monster saw his pray. He grabbed the boy, and strangalled him, he ground his bones, and pulled out his eyes, sucked his blood and gobbed his head like scrambbed eggs. He is still waiting for an inisent child so don't go wandering again.

Stuart then rewrites this section as follows:

He grabbed the boy/with his grewsome, hairy arms,/he strangalled the insent boy/and poped out his eyes. riped his head off. ate his brains like

toffee eggs. He drunk his blood while eating. He is still waiting maybe for you.

Underneath, probably after consultation with his teacher, he has written "gruesome, innocent, strangled."

Stuart's final version, written in noticeably neater handwriting than any of the previous versions reads:

> **Midnight in a misty graveyard.**
> **A hairy thing.**
> **A gruesome thing was lurking.**
> **Just waiting for his pray.**
> **A small boy was running.**
> **The monster saw his pray.**
> **He grabbed the boy**
> **With his gruesome hairy arms.**
> **He strangled the innocent boy.**
> **He poped out his eyes, ripped his**
> **Head off. Ate his brains like toffee eggs.**
> **He drunk his blood while eating.**
> **He is still waiting...maybe for you.**

A very "average" piece of writing you might say, but then Stuart probably regards himself (at best!) as a very "average" writer. What can be tracked here, because we have the whole writing journey, are the improvements that he made as he reconsidered each piece and then rewrote it. I would suggest that it is important for Stuart to be able to take note of these improvements—along with his teacher and also his parents, if pupils' work is available for consideration on parents' evenings. As I have said elsewhere and will repeat—our benchmark for progress should be where the pupil *starts from* not where we expect him to finish.

Poems That Came from Clusters

This class of eleven-year-olds had never tried clustering before as a means of collecting ideas and images that could then be thought about further. We started very simply by taking a color—red, and making a joint free-associational cluster on the blackboard. Once the class had caught on to the idea of a "magnet word" that attracts all sorts of meanings to it, everyone had a go doing their own cluster for "white." After a minute or two ideas were shared in pairs and I then suggested that each writer expand four or five cluster associations by writing a whole line for each one. Raymond wrote:

> **White is walls in a hospital.**
> **White is a wedding dress.**
> **White is sheets on my bed.**
> **White is Elephants running in the Jungle.**

White is drawing paper or writing paper.
White is the clouds in the sky.
White is a rubber.
White is paint in a pot.
White is a silky polar bear.

Everyone then chose their favorite line and we had a read around the class. Here are some of them:

White is walls in a hospital.
White is paint bright and shiny.
White is hair of an old age pair.
White is a ghost who wanders round the attic.
Snow is white like a sheet of paper lying on the ground.
White is snowdrop lovely.
White is a swan gliding silently across a lake.

Perhaps because it was the Armistice Week, and because the original "red" cluster had produced associations such as "blood" and "poppies," I next asked the class to cluster individually again, using the magnet word "war." They then spent a longer stretch of time free writing and experimenting with various versions, culminating in a final fair copy—mostly accompanied by a small neat illustration.

Raymond

Raymond had jotted down a very simple cluster which contained these chains of single words: "Bombs, Army/Battles/Planes, Tanks/Soildier/Guns/ Weapons, Bullets/Ships/Seargent." His first free write came as something of a surprise after this basic list:

(1) I was up to my neck in mud.
and I was covered in blood.
And when the Germans invided.
We invaded Back.
it was bad war is sad.
and war is not glad.

Raymond then crossed through the whole of this draft with two large crosses and wrote quite a different second version:

(2) BOOM . BOOM . BOOM .
The world is coming to its Doom
There's fiting here theres fiting in Germany
wy is there so many enamys
All we want is PEACE
But the war will not come to a cease

He seemed better pleased with these lines but in his third and final piece, he has both extended from here and also paid closer attention to the overall rhythm:

(3) Boom, Boom, Boom,
the world is coming to its Doom.
There's fighting here.
There's fighting there.
There's fighting Everywere
All we want is peace
But the war will not cease
The guns are fired
And the men are hired

Adrian

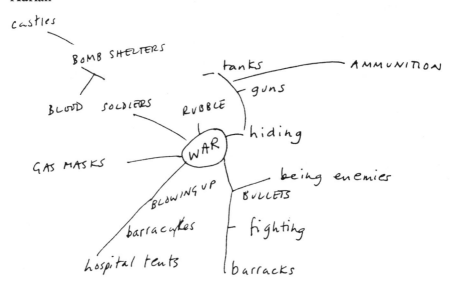

Figure 6–13   Adrian's Initial Cluster

Figure 6–13 shows Adrian's initial cluster. After this his first two extensions were very prosaic, focusing mainly on "BLOWING UP" and its aftereffects:

(1) As the battle ceased I went out, there was a lot of rubble and hospital tents blown up by tanks and missiles. I was scared The Plane was shot down that I had been flying. it was wrecked.

(2) As the battle ceased i went out, there was a lot of rubble and nobody about. Hospital tents blasted by tanks and missiles. I could see the smoke for miles and miles. why does war always start up, the crockery and the cups are all blown up, dead people in the trenches grunting and groaning and rats roaming how could this thing start up

In this second version, Adrian has discovered a rhythm which he retains in his third and fourth versions, giving it an added emphasis by picking it out in distinct lines:

(3) As the battle ceased I went out,
There was a lot of rubble and nobody about,
Hospital tents blasted by tanks and missiles,
I could see the smoke for miles and miles,
The crockery and cups all blown up!
dead people [crossed out] Dying men in trenches grunting and groaning,
Rats roaming. why does war always have to start?

(4) As the battle ceased I went out,
There was a lot of rubble and nobody about,
Hospital tents blasted by tanks and missiles,
I could see the smoke for miles and miles.
Dying men in trenches grunting and groaning,
Rats roaming.
Why does war always have to start?

I'm interested that Adrian is willing to cut out the cups and crockery from his final version, but retains "Rats roaming" as a strong short line on its own.

A Twelve-Year-Old Compiles His Own Writing Journey

These middle school pupils knew before they began their journeys, that they would be keeping each stage—along with their own comments and those of their response partners in a large construction-paper book which literally showed their thinking from start to finish. I find the running alongside of their own comments with those of their response partners, particularly interesting, especially in this case! The whole class had begun from the same starting point—a clustering of their associations with the magnet word "fear."

I have chosen Paul's journey partly because it resulted in his writing a much longer newspaper article than computer software programs usually seem to encourage, and partly because he includes in his account some lively badinage between himself and one of his correspondents. In his rough writing his spelling is frequently inventive; in his article (which is not revised), the change to more standard spelling is quite marked. By that stage we can see how his ideas had been worked out in some detail. Paul can afford therefore to give some attention to code as well as to product—and it pays off. His cluster is shown in Figure 6–14. Here are Paul's comments on his clustering and his partner's response:

I have writen many fears people have. I shared my comments that I had writen on my cluster. We were able to exchange idears very quickly and

Figure 6–14   Paul's Cluster

at first my own idears did'ent come to fast but I started with **strangers** and then expanded on my idears. I started with things like reptiles, then fears of destasters—Aids, nuclar desasters and then less important things such as forgetting home work.

My Partner's comments [after discussion?]:
(Robert) I think Paul has coverd more than one thing in each subject. But could expand on what he has done and filled "in between the lines a bit" and given a bit more information.

In his "Rough Write 1," Paul made a list of "Possible lines for a newspaper story" as follows:

Strangers, Nuclar war, Homework, Aids, Insects, Snakes, Dentist, Lifts, Confined spaces, Fear of the dark.
After looking at the above possible story lines I decided on these five. 1) Homework, 2) Dentist, 3) Lifts, 4) Confined spaces, 5) Fear of the dark.

Rough Write 2

A girl wakes up one day and remembers some unfinished homework. Quickly rushes it off and gets into trouble.

A man goes to his dentenst and he has many worries, and the dentist makes a terrible mastake.

A woman wents into a lift with three other people and the lift breaks down.

A man worked for the secret surface and was caught on an operation and got put into a small room and goes mad!

A child has a terrible fear of an evil goblin under its bed.

Comments from Paul's second responder:

You have had sufficient experience of the possible first three story lines that you have chosen and I would think that your imagination will give you ample ammunition for either of the last two. Whichever you choose, the story should be at least interesting.

Paul adds: "I think the comments are quite fair."

Final Rough Write

The story of the man with a fear of confined spaces.
1. Mans backround.
   Mr Chapmans umbrella was still left from when he was last at Dr Kills prision; he is a secret sirface agent.
2. He is standing in a railway station waiting for another tip off from a fellow agent. As a train comes into the station.
3. Two KILL againts grab Mr Chapman and take him to KILL agents HQ in a car. He is met by Mr Kill.
4. When he refuses to answere questions about the secret surfas he is tourcherd by being put into a confined room.
5. Slowly but surely he goes mad and Goverment agents finally loclate Mr Chapman's Prison –
6. and rescue him but it is too late!

Anthony's response:

Paul had some good points but should change his way of writing it.

Paul's reply:

Yes, I think I should set my work out more sensiblay.

Robert's response:

I think that Paul has mised the point of the work. Im not sure what the numbers are for but it probaly means something to him. Im also not sure what the umbrella is for in the story he sais its for decoration. The story could do with a bit more "filling in" when he does it in neat. The secret agent going mad is an odd ingredient in the story that is very unfilled in. I shall be interested to see the final result.

Paul's reply:

I have not quiet missed the point but mearly added some variaty to this project. The umbrella was mearly put in to add to the readers picture of the seen. The numbers are put in to show when the sentence is finished. Robert says that my story needs more filling in but I must remind Robert that this is only a rough write and not the final draf. I hope that he will read my final draft as he promissed.

Paul's lead newspaper story:

[In banner headlines in red]

22nd March   M.I.5. LEAK—MADMAN AT THE CENTER OF A K.I.L.L. PLOT!

An amazing plot was decovered by the Daily News yesterday. A Mr Chapman who has now gone mad was waiting by a railway line when he was abducted by K.I.L.L. agents. The entire story can be read today and tomorrow...Mr K.I.L.L. tells all...! "Mr Chapman was waiting by a railway line, waiting for another agent when my men came up to him and took him to K.I.L.L. HQ." "How did you get him there?" "My men took him into a car, which took him to our HQ, an underground tube station abonanded for some unknown reason.

We knew that Mr Chapman had a fear of confined spaces and so we thretened him with fire, water and pain making devices but he resested them all...I don't know what came over me, but I suddenly wanted him dead..." "Why did you want him dead?" "I found that I could not get any secrets out of him...!"

He was then taken away from Highworth Police Station Prision and into court where the Jury is going to decide his future. The second part of this story is in tomorrow's addition.

Sport

Everton are doing very well in the Barclays Bank Leage—who are running a competition to design the cup for the winers.

I have no doubt that this "item" was added to Paul's lead story to make his front page look more authentic. The writing was presented in columns to look like a newspaper. On a further page Paul wrote (in banner headlines in red):

23rd March   Part 2 of our MI5 STORY

Following up yesterdays story about Mr K.I.L.L. who kidnaped secret agents and unless they told the secrects of Great Britain they would go mad.

"So how did the Jury find you, guilty or not guilty?" "Guilty." "I can only talk for a few minutes." One last thing—how did Mr Chapman go mad? "We put him in a small room and he slowly went mad!" "What does K.I.L.L. stand for?" K = Killing I = ingering L = lieing and L = leaking! "I see, well how long have you got?" 20 years—19 if I am lucky!

Interview by Paul Hillier M.B.E.

Unfortunately there is no record of any further comments from either of Paul's correspondents but my guess is that they would both have approved of the way he had expanded on his final rough write when he came to produce his article. True it would have benefited from an editorial proofread, but the zestful interview with Mr K.I.L.L. has a journalistic feel about it which is well captured for a twelve-year-old—and as I commented earlier, it is considerably longer than any news items that I have seen produced for the computer programs Front Page or Fleet Street. I especially like the continuation on the second day—after the jury have given their verdict.

Finding a Place to Start From

For this writing journey the 3rd-year class (aged thirteen to fourteen) were first asked to do a minute's brainstorming to collect a list of as many places as they could think of that they had actually visited or lived in.

Next they each chose from their list the place they would most like to be. Switching into *picture thinking*, everyone wrote down two or three clear images or snapshots of the place each had chosen. Next each person drew a *sketch map* of the place—or part of it. They then *free wrote* for a paragraph or so about their recollected feelings—and did a final free write about any *people* they connected with this place. By the time these activities were completed, the seventy-minute-long lesson was at an end.

In the next lesson, the teacher suggested a variety of forms for everyone to consider before embarking on a continuous piece of writing: story; play; newspaper report; one day in . . . ; good times, bad times; description— prose or poetry; diary entry. Stories and descriptions in both prose and poetry turned out to be the most popular forms. I have chosen one poem, one story and one autobiographical description from the writings which emerged from this sequence of exploratory activities.

Each pupil in this class produced only a first draft; one can only speculate therefore on any editorial changes they might have made given the opportunity for just one rewrite.

Charlotte

Charlotte chose a place from her list that she had visited more than once because she had relations there—Selby, in the North of England. These are her preliminary thoughts:

1. **The first picture is of Selby Abbey, its 4 facing towers with a clock on each face, the hands made of a gold plated metal, the building made of stone.**
2. **The park of Selby with its bandstand in the middle surrounded by flowers and trees, grass laying between each patch of flowers. The cafe near by with the ice-cream sign outside and a hanging basket filled with blue and red flowers.**
3. **On the outskirts of the town lies a forest on a hill, the trees sloping symetricaly towards the centre. Paths leading up towards a wooden fence and a wooden gate, there are no trees for a few meters, then there is the occasional oak with its' leaves towering above the ground.**

After she had drawn her map here is what Charlotte wrote about her feelings and about "people" :

I like to go to Selby because the people there are very friendly, they aren't posh, they're very helpful. We go to Selby because my Nan lives in a very small town just outside and sometimes you see occaisional dog running around. The shops provide us with all that we need, and the

abbey is the main attraction, sittuated at the top of the street, it looks very pretty.

The person I asociate with Selby is my Nan. She has lived there all her life. When my parents walked the south Penine Way I stayed with, I was very young at the time and can remember her giving me some sweets and telling me stories. Sometimes I went next door to play with the children next door.

Some further "reflections":

This little town is a peaceful place. The market provides fresh fruit and veg at a resonable price. Selby has amenities which are needed by all of the town folk.

The park and the swimming pool provide a place to go for the young-sters. The swimming pool is quite large and is indoors. It is situated out of the town center.

The train station provides a regular run from London to York which by-passes Selby.

Charlotte's continuous draft:

There are shops which are very good for souvenirs and include pieces of information about the abbey. This is the main atraction, it is very old and some locals believe that it is slowly but surely sinking, the river which runs nearby is called the River Oose. The abbey has been visited by several royal people. Each point of the compass has a facing door, for example East Wing. The "towers" all contain a clock and every hour on the hour the bells ring, a chime which can be heard all over the town. The clock has Roman numerals as numbers and they look very elegant as they shine in the middaysun. The doors are made out of solid oak wood and against the stone walls it looks very pretty. The abbey is in the middle of a mini-park with a few trees and flowerbeds around it. In the summer when the flowers are out the abbey looks very picturesque.

The people who live in Selby have a very strong Yorkshire accent, and welcome any visitors to their county. When people think of Yorkshire they see two steriotypes. The first being cobbled streets, old houses and men with flat caps smoking pipes. The second being all factories and power and coal plants "littering" the countryside. Smoke rising and polluting the air.

Yorkshire is a very pretty county in places and the Penine way takes you along the prettiest countryside that I've ever seen. Waterfalls, streams, hills and valleys all go to make up Yorkshire.

Charlotte added as a footnote:

I chose to write about Selby in a description because it tells you more about the place especially if you go into great detail.

Kerry

Kerry put three ticks on her brainstormed places list against Porton, a small village not far from her school. Kerry was clearly a fast writer as her preliminary "short burst writings" are increasingly extensive:

1. Porton—small stream, island, bridge, ducks, frogs, fields with cows, trees, muddy bank.
2. There is an old house with a big garden, with snowdrops dotted around. There is a big willow tree and pigeons are sat in it.
3. There are lots of fields, differently colored, There is a railway track with bushes growing wild around it. There is a bridge going over what once was a stream but has dried up. There are cows grazing and horses running.
4. There is a trickling stream with ducks on it and on the small bridge are frogs but only a couple. There is an island in this stream. It has trees and flowers on it. The only way to get there is by walking across a fallen tree, which is slippery because muddy boots have been across it. There are birds singing and the whole scenery is quiet-looking and typical of the countryside.

My feelings about Porton

Porton is relaxing and peaceful. When I go there I feel as if my whole character changes and I'm someone else. The people are friendly and they all seem to be animal lovers. When I go to Porton the air seems somehow different and fresh. The atmosphere is friendly and I really look forward to going there. It makes a pleasant change to look out onto fields instead of traffic and noise. In Porton, outside is a different world altogether and the air makes my appetite grow and I often walk around, looking at the scenery.

People

My grandad lives in Porton and I often associate him with there. He has a character which all people in Porton seem to have. He is jolly, always joking, and as he is a farmer this means that he works hard and eats heartily. He usually makes fun of me but it's always good-naturedly. He lives in a farmhouse which seems old (as do most houses there) but cosy and welcoming and that welcome I associate with him, and others who live in Porton.

For her draft poem (in which there are just three crossings out) Kerry wrote:

Runaway

Racing along the deserted street,
Tense with excitement and fear,
Listening intently for the sound of feet,
Or for my parents or the Police to appear.

Running over the bridge, with fresh fields all around
And the clean cold air whipping at my face,
The ducks I have woken make a familiar sound,
One welcoming thing in any case.
The railway track is rumbling slightly,
That is a sure sign,
That the midnight train's coming, lights shining
                                        brightly.
It whistles loudly, shrilly, to call out that it's
                                        on time.

That danger's over,
I've not been spotted,
I get up from the damp clover,
My hair very knotted.
I race up to an old house
And ring the bell, feeling bold,
And stand at the door, nervous as a mouse,
but shivering vigorously in the cold.
The door opens and a woman stands there,
Her voice kindly cooing like a dove,
And as I explain she listens, doesn't stare,
And I recognize her character, and this place is full
                                        of love.

David

David didn't in fact make use of any of his preliminary writings! He started with two brief word-pictures of Salisbury, drew a vague map which could have been anywhere—then switched to Boscombe Down where he lived and wrote "I think it is a very nice place to live in, lots of people to make friends with." He wrote nothing further about people however; that was it. Hardly a promising start!

From the choice of forms offered by the teacher, David chose to write a story which he called "A Crossroads Crash" :

Eating my dinner on a cold Autumn Afternoon I was thinking how exiting it would be to see an accident on our road. Then lots of questions went through my head, would there be any blood? Would there be any dead people lying accross the road? What would I do if I saw one? Should I help the injured or go for help? Should I phone the emergency service or wait for someone else to do it? I started to throw all these questions at my mum but all I got back was, "I doubt wether there'll be any chrash round here," and, "Even if there was I doubt wether you'll be there so just eat your dinner, then you can take the dog for a walk."

I thought it was useless talking to her, it's like talking to a cup of tea! So I decided to work it out whilst taking the dog for a walk.

I arrived at the point where I thought would be the most likely place for an accident, a fast crossroads where cars are coming and going.

I decided to sit on a bench about ten yards away from the road. I looked around for a telephone box to see how far I had to go if I had to phone an ambulance or whatever, next I looked around for nearby houses. All these things were within 200 yards of the crossroads. I felt much reasured now that Ive got all this sorted out, I calld the dog, put him back on the lead, and walked home.

Next day I walked over to the crossroads to see if the telephone box had run away or the houses decided to take off, but they were all still there.

Suddenly there was a [*flash* crossed out] loud crash. I looked to see what happened but was blinded by a red flash, I opened my eyes again to see a blue mini go flying through the air, I looked to where the flash came from I saw an articulated lorry coming to a halt on top of another mini, then all was still, I went round all the vehicals to see if anybody was fit enough to come and help me with the injured. There wasn't, so I ran to the nearest house, there was no need everybody had run out to see what happened.

About five minutes later the ambulance came to pick up the injured, the break down came a bit later to pick up the vehicals.

I told my mum all about it, she didn't believe me.

I am intrigued by each of these pupil's drafts—and by the degree to which each in its own way has been "shaped at the point of utterance," to use Britton's phrase. Undoubtedly each could have been improved with a little careful proofreading and perhaps line realignment. But I cannot imagine that any of the writers would have made any major editorial changes. I would want to hypothesize that having time to enter into these landscapes first, to put into words their first images, to "map" the place as they drew and to reflect about their feelings and about the people, helped Charlotte and Kerry to write fluently when it came to their continuous draft.

But David had written hardly anything, prior to launching into his story and yet it has a vigor which moves the reader forward at a good pace. It also made me smile more than once. Perhaps David had indeed been over this possible scenario as he walked the dog—who is to say. But I quote his story here as a reminder that we can never predict what will emerge from head to page—and discovering from someone else's suggestions what you DON'T want to write about can sometimes lead you to the very thing!

Winter Poem—in Response to a Text

The poem that follows comes from a 4th-year secondary class. After the initial brainstorm to recollect whatever images of winter came immediately to mind, the class were then asked to brainstorm more specifically on the effects that winter had on human beings and other creatures. Both sets of recollections were shared with partners and some with the whole class.

The teacher then read the following poem by Judith Nicholls out loud:

Winter

Winter crept
through the whispering wood,
hushing fir and oak;
crushed each leaf and froze each web—
but never a word he spoke.

Winter prowled
by the shivering sea,
lifting sand and stone;
nipped each limpet silently—
and then moved on.

Winter raced
down the frozen stream,
catching at his breath;
on his lips were icicles—
at his back was death.

The children were invited to refer back to their own brainstorms and to have a go at reconstructing them into a poetic form. Most were happy to experiment with their own word-shaping through two or three drafts. Only Royston, who would never have regarded himself as among the more literary members of the class, was influenced by Nicholls' use of personification. His poem is the more powerful as a result.

Royston

Quick brainstorm

darkness and howlling wind pluse snow and the crisp icey crunch of snow and death and bitter cold and the icey roads and grite. and home sweet home warm and inviting vesters [?] at the house. draft[?] people geting head on the slaging slope. cliserosion[?] starvation

The effects of winter

the darness of winter can stope you cole. the howlling wind thunder around the sole of a beird and can banny(?) a car. The ice and the snow are the masters of dissection. Cars are sliding round and round and the air is stile. other sielance can be dakend with the howlling of death and deruction. So you runaway.

First draft [After listening to Nicholls' poem]

the man of ice he walks on air.
The slow silent foot steaps [and yet crossed out] so strong
The blinding snow as wite as the cape of silk which flows behide his back
The dead of cold and thunder that lashes out and seses the frale and week
It clings like a calis on his back.

Oh how he will try to scrape it off.
Poor man of ice.
Which hides the shado of death.

Second draft

The man of ice he walks on air
The slow and silant foot steap so strong.
The blinding snow as wite as the cape
of snow which flows from his back.
The cape which hides the shadow of death.

The dead of cold persists
the bones of the old and weak.
The death which cold doth bring sises the old and fraile
and flowts them away into the darkness of death.
It clings like a canker on his back,
Oh how he will try to scrape it off.
Poor man of the ice.

Richard's Story: "Vicar"

Richard, in another 4th-year secondary class, started with a brainstorm on different kinds of windows. Amongst others on his initial list he included "cracked window, French window, dirty window and stane glass window." He then chose one of these windows to cluster further ideas from as shown in Figure 6–15. After this cluster, he wrote down two lists of "opposites" to suggest ideas that might create tension in a story—as yet to be invented (see Figure 6–16). He then, in a short piece of free writing, produced the following ideas which he shared orally with a small group of friends:

Could be a poem showing the contrast of inside a church and the busy life outside. It could be a story of a vicar and his fight for peace in the community. Could be a poem about a man sitting inside a church or

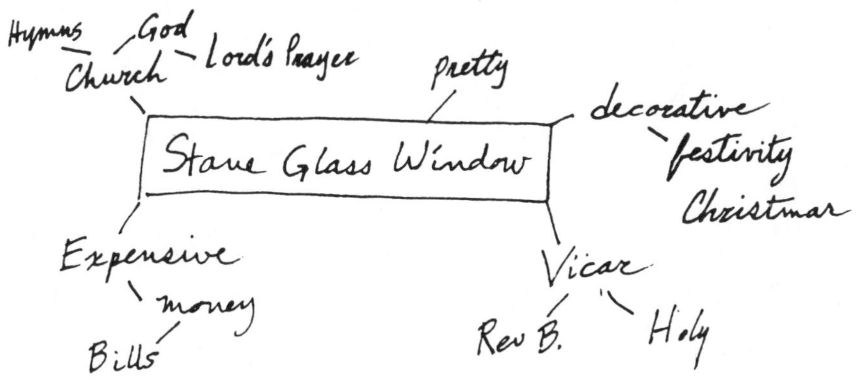

Figure 6–15   Richard's Cluster

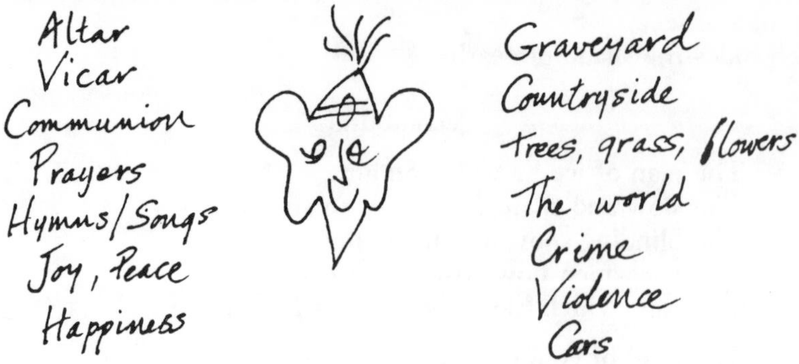

Figure 6-16   Richard's List of Opposites

in an empty Town Street. He may witness some violent crime. He would realize the corruption of the world. The man could even be a vicar.

After discussion, Richard's further short free write reads:

It is about a vicar who is in a world of his own. He does not see the violence and hatred. I would like the story to shorten a bit and become a bit more descriptive. He goes out to the streets to find out what life is really like and sees violent crime and attacks [?] which make him very scared. In the end he vanishes into nowhere.

After these preliminaries, Richard then produced the following (unedited) story:

Oh God

He sat there transfixed, unable to speak, a deathly white color. He was sweating and shaking. In the light falling through the staned glass window the dust swirled as if it were dancing. His hands met and joined together. He mumbled a prayer over and over again. He remembered that morning and what had happened. He shut his eyes and screwed up his face unable to shut the thoughts of the day from his mind. He cried.

It was 9.30. As usual the happy figure of a man dressed in black robes walked along the path nodding his head and saying "Good morning my child" to any person he happened to pass. As he reached the gate he fumbled in his pocket for the keys that would unlock the great wooden doors.

The Reverent Browning had been vicar of the parish for as long as anybody cared to remember. He was possibly the nicest man you could ever meet. He generally tidied round the little church and then went home but today was different. After he had finished his little jobs he went to the altar and started to pray deeply.

In the past he had been accused of burying his head in the sand over controversial subjects like abortion, sex education and particurly crime and violence. Every time he was taken on one side he muttered and fumbled excuses as if frightened to mention such things. He was in a world of his own.

As he kneeled down he suddenly noticed the cold chill that had developed in the church since he had been there. He scurried along the pews towards the doors to see if they had come ajar. As he approached them he was startled to hear a loud but kindly voice. "Return to the altar" it said, "Who's there?" shouted the reverent slightly disturbed by the loudness of the voice. "Come sit at the altar and I will tell you." Reverent Browning did as he was asked and went to the altar and stood.

What happened next was undoubtedly a miracle in the true sense of the word. As he stood there particles of light rushed at each other until a solid mass had formed. From this an apparition of an old man appeared. The old man opened his arms as if in a gesture of greeting. "I am the Lord God" he said. The vicar fell to his knees trembling with fear and joy. "If only you would listen to your brothers and sisters" the old man continued. "If you opened your eyes you would see the hatred and contempt of this world", he bowed his head as if in shame "that I created. Go out and see for yourself. If you do not you will never know what this world is really like." The old man smiled and as quickly as he had appeared the glowing image disappeared.

One hour later he was seen leaving the small church. He went quickly and silently towards the busy center of the town that lay within a mile of the church. He sat on a bench and observed as much as he could as soon as he got there. Some of the sights he saw disturbed him. One of the first things he witnessed was two eight year old boys pick-pocketing an old lady. He saw people fighting in the streets. In the afternoon he saw a robery taking place. The gun, the screams, the shot. He was beggining to realize. As the evening drew ever nearer and the town became less crowded he saw a terrible thing. A group of youths had collected outside an amusement arcade. They seemed to be smoking cigarette like objects but he knew not what they were. Some had different colored hair and studded leather jackets with obsceneties written all over the backs. In the distance an old lady limped towards them. The gang smiled and walked in the direction that she was coming in. As she tried to walk around them they set about her. Reverent Browning heard the thumping, kicking, muffled screams. "No" he yelled and ran at the mob. He dived into them and landed next to the bloodied remains of the old lady. Her body moved in spasms as she lay dieing.

The siren rang its warning as the car came speeding through the streets. The mob had already dissapeared. Not knowing what to do he got up and looked down at the old lady. He ran away as the first puddles of blood trickled down into the gutter. He ran all the way back to the church stopping to talk to nobody.

As the sun sank down below the horizon casting its remaining light on the land a man sat crying in a church. Slowly he raised himself and stumbled to the altar, shouting at the roof "Oh God, I have seen the real world, the hatred and violence, take me please."

Ten years later Inspector Barnes was looking through all the old files. He moved to the unfound section. Pulled out a file and looked at a paper on top of all the others. As he glanced across it he felt a curiosity. Apparently a Reverent Browning had gone missing and never been found. All they ever recovered were his robes and his Bible that were left lying on the altar in a heap. The incident had happened on the night of a brutal attack on an old lady. I wonder if that's a coincidence the Chief Inspector thought to himself.

The End

I am intrigued by this story—and by the confidence of the draft. The time sequencing, from the evening, back through the events of the day, returning to that same evening—and then through a ten-year leap to the Inspector reflecting on the unsolved mystery, is smoothly handled. The tale is told simply—with the occasional striking of a religious chord ("he knew not what they were . . . "). The priest's innocence is brutally destroyed but the writer avoids flamboyance and sentimentality, preferring understatement if anything: "As the sun sank down below the horizon . . . a man sat crying in a church." The ambivalence of the Inspector's final thoughts conclude the tale on a wry note.

But the piece does have a prehistory and I find that intriguing too. There is the initial brainstorm which produces the image of a stained glass window on which Richard focuses for his cluster and which makes one colorful appearance in the opening paragraph of the story: "In the light falling through the staned glass window the dust swirled as if it were dancing."

The brainstorm for "opposites" provides Richard with his literal inner microcosm of the church contrasted to the world outside as well as with the introspective inner life of the priest compared with the turbulence of a corrupt world.

Then there are the two short pieces of free writing, the first of which is discussed with others in the class and the second shared with the teacher. The seeds which blossom in the story are all there in the first free write although at this stage Richard is still undecided as to whether he will choose poem or story as his form. The sense of playing upon contrasting scenes and feelings is strongly present. In his second brief free write after small-group discussion, the writer is much more definite about his intentions— and about the basic outline of the plot which has now taken shape.

The point I want to make is that Richard was encouraged by the strategies that his teacher suggested, to prepare the ground before he drafted. By the time he wrote the opening paragraph of his story some important decisions had been made which helped him to keep the narrative in focus. It is exceptionally successful as a first continuous draft.

Editing for Meaning: Greg's Story

I have chosen to set the whole of Greg's original draft against his edited version as I believe that his revision indicates clearly the considerable improvements that can be made to a one-off piece of writing if only pupils can be given the encouragement and the time to rethink. Already I can hear the heartfelt cry from British teachers and students alike: *But what about the folders?* My question is this—is it better to extort one "finished" piece a fortnight from students, thus rendering any careful rethinking unrealistic if not impossible, while at the same time assessing the student's performance only on first efforts (an assessment that any professional writer would regard as an insult); or is it better to continue to make the case—as strongly and with whatever evidence we can provide, that producing fewer finished pieces actually improves the quality of those which are produced?

Greg's Original Draft: *What Happened to Him?*

The water rushed onwards, moving towards a plunging, foaming waterfall. Spray richochets from the water hitting the rocks. The pool below is green, deep and defending of its own treasures, the surface is constantly moving. Further on down the stream the water is quiter. It moves slowly between its [?] walls, the bottom is gravely, a few fish are moving around, but otherwise the stream is lifeless.

The Drizzle comes down like a Solid Wall, Covering everything, except for the man who sits contentedly in the shed beside the stream. A small fire burns, the man Sits Contentedly munching away on a large chocolate bar. He is dressed raggedly with a tweed coat, tied around the waste with a peice of String, underneath he wears a thick grey jumper. His trousers are brown and he wears Gum boots. His hair is Surprisingly neat, Cut very short at the back and Sides, with the hair on the top of his head closely cropped and brushed to one side.

Unlike many tramps and wanderers he drinks water, and he is very clean. Beside him sits a small dog, his tongue hanging out, his eyes are keen and alert, wiry hair covers his face. While the rest of his body is covred in soft hair.

Greg's Revised Version: *Mystery on the Moors*

The water rushed onward, moving toward a plunging, foaming waterfall. Spray evolved by the water hitting the rocks, it turned into a rainbow. Below the pool carved from the rock by the continuous beating of the water, is emerald green, the surface is broken by the cascading water. Further on down the rivers course the water is quiter and more slowly moving.

The drizzle comes down in soaking blankets covering everything, except for the man that sits in a little hut, he is leant against the wall chomping a chocolate bar. He is dressed raggedly with a tweed coat hung about his frame, underneath he wears a thick grey jumper. His trousers are brown and bordering on being too short, they look almost tailor made for him. His large clompy boots look decidedly out of place against his trousers.

One factor stands out about his appearance, his hair, it is closely cropped and brushed to one side. Thus giving him a certain elegance, against his clothing. He drinks from a flask, and he is immaculatly clean. Beside him sits a dog, his tongue lolls around his open mouth, his eyes are keen and alert. Wiry hair his head and face while his body hair is short and soft.

Elsewhere a group of three walkers troop towards home, all three of them are dressed in Bright orange with their compasses hanging around their necks. They are singing, their voices ring around the hills on any other day, but with the sheets of rain comeing down, their voices are muffled. The leader strides onward looking very confident and matter of fact. The person behind him is tired and stumbling. His complaints are louder than the [?] from the other two. While the person at the back of the group is singing loudly, his whole manner suggests he is a very alive and jumpy get up and go person. Soon their calm assurance, complaining, singing voices are swallowed in the squall.

A few miles off a man is getting ready to go out, the river next to his shelter is now gaining speed and power, eating the banks away like a hungry animal. The dog shifts from left to right, his tail wags, he waits for his master to leave. Finally after checking that everything is in order the man stands. The dog looks up and up, the man seems to uncoil, he rises and rises until he can go no further, he stands at least 6′ 4″. The dog now seems as if he is going to jump out of his skin he's so excited, the man looks down and pats the dog gently. "Later" he said, "later."

The darkness begins to close in as he leaves the safety of his shed, the grass is wet and slippy, the man seems to find it hard to stand. Just as he reaches a style he slips and falls. Curses flow readily from his pain contorted lips, he lays for a while, then with a great effort he pulls himself up. His hand oozes blood, he takes a peice of cloth from a pocket and stems the rush of blood, doggedly he carries on.

The man stands and [slides?] out of the protection of the hut to relieve himself. Not more than 50 yards away a group of walkers pass. There step is springy except for one who keeps slipping and sliding. There bright orange waterproof clothing is darkened in patches where the rain has been to much for it.

They are singing as they march homeward toward their hired house. On any other day their voices ring around the hills, but not this day, the voices die on the wind and rain. The leader strides forth, an air of confidence seems to surround him. Behind a man struggles, he slips and curses between verses of the song. The person at the back of the group is singing loudly and walking with a step full of exuberance. Soon their voices die and the man re-enters his hut.

The man again readies himself to leave the shelter of the hut. The river next to the hut is now growing and it eats the banks away like a hungry animal. Inside the hut the dog shifts from side to side, his tail wags furiously, he waits for his master to leave. The man stands, his great height seems to make him look even less like the tramp he appears to be. The dog is so excited it seems he is going to take off in a flying leap toward his master. The man bends and pats the dog on the back of the head "later" he says "later"

The darkness begins to close in as he leaves the safety of the hut the long grass is made slippy by the shroud of drizzle, the man is uninhibited he moves quitely and easily over it, but surprisingly he falls and lands heavily, he curses violently, but seems unhurt. Doggedly he gets up and gets over the stile.

The noise as he moves off dies,

Behind him where he fell a possesion has been lost. A gust of wind blows the leather wallet open. Inside is the man's identity. Surprisingly for a supposed tramp the wallet is quite full, mainly with money and pictures of a woman relaxing near a swimming pool. The house in the background is large, green plants entwine with the nests against the house. The small dog can be seen lying just behind the chair in which the woman sits. Soon the picture is obscured by the drops of water from the sky. Contained in a small pocket hidden away back of the wallet is the mans true identity. It reads Harvey Johnson B.Sc. O.B.E. Proffessor of Chemical industries. Behind this card it has another card. Director of a Chemical Company. So why if this man was doing so well for himself would he wish to hide away in a small shed in the middle of November.

The room was warm and cosy, the log fire burned brightly, omitting just enough light for the room to be visible. Old and comfortable furniture gives the room a certain character, a thick brown shagpile matches the furniture perfectly. A large lamp stands in one corner of the room. below it is a small bookshelf, holding books such as the outdoor handbook and the illustrated guide to Britain. Obviously this is a reading corner. The old chair suggests the reading corner is not for show. Elsewhere in the room there is a huge old cabinet, containing cut crystall glasses and a variety of spirits. A small television set stands in the corner of the room opossite to that of the bookshelf and lamp. Grouped around the television are the three walkers.

Phil a medium sized man points

to who's competing to make the most noise. Suddenly a gust of wind decides who wins the competition, but this is not all that it does, a peice of leather is turned over on the ground, it reveals the mans identity. Surprisingly the wallet is quite full, mainly with money, but nestling behind the money is a picture of a woman, she sits beside a pool, beneath her feet is the little dog from the hut.

The picture becomes obscured by the constant wetness from the heavens, behind this is a small pocket containing two pieces of card. On one card the mans name and credentials are written, by the evidence from it he is an important and clever man. The second card has its back to the front of the wallet, it looks as if it has been hidden, it proclaims that this man is a director of a large company. But why would he be out on the moors like this, that is if they are his cards.

The room is warm and cosy, the log fire burns brightly, omitting just enough light to allow the room to be visible. Old and comfy furnidhings give the room a certain antiquated charm, a thick brown shagpile matches the furniture perfectly. A large lamp stands in the corner of the room, the bulb is not lit but the light from the fire is enough to illuminate the small bookshelf below it. A large armchair sits next to it, the cushion is indented with the shape of someone's back. This suggests the reading corner is not for show, but that it is often used. Elsewhere in the room there is a large cabinet, inside this is a set of cut crystall glasses, beside them stands a bottle of whiskey, a fine old brand that explains the presence of the glasses.

A small television stands in one corner of the room, grouped around out in no uncertain terms that the program they are whatching is Rubbish. Yanni a tall gangly fellow who seems to be of mediterranean origin mumbles something inconceivable, while Shuan a chunky man of medium height sits contentedly eating his dinner and saying the program is fun and livly. Their hair is wet and a dryer rumbles in the background. Soon they begin to talk of the day just gone by. It is plain to see that Phil is the leader, Yanni the reluctant and confused follower and Shaun is the beans of the group, cheerful and chatty.

After about an hour of talking Phil decides to go to bed, saying he wants to be up bright and early for tomorrows expedition. After about ten minutes Yanni follows. Shaun is alone, brooding over the day. Something clicks in his mind, he remembers seeing a man near the old hut at the stream. He found this very strange as the man had no walking equipment and he certainly wasn't dressed for walking. He looked like a tramp but that was immposible they were 50 miles from any other human Habitation. But soon the idea of the man being anything more than a tramp was dismissed. Shaun picked up the paper and began to read the Sports page. The headline of the paper read "Brilliant Chemical Scientist goes missing."

Only a few hundred yards away the man moved onward through the long grass of the feild directly behind the house. His hand was now bound tightly by a rag of clothing. His movements were quick and easy, little noise could be heard as he moved across the field.

Inside the house Shuan had finally decided to go to bed. He switched off the reading lamp and

this are the three walkers. Phil a medium sized man, with a hard set face and eyes that are filled with a kind of superiority points out that in his opinion the programme they are whatching is childish rubbish. Yanni a tall gangly man that seems to be of mediterranean origin mutters something incomprehensible. While beside him Shaun sits, eating his dinner and at the same time arguing that the programme is fun and livly. Their hair is wet and the noise of a dryer can be heard rumbling in the background. Soon they begin to talk of the day that they have just had. Phil seems to believe that it could have been better and he is obviously the leader. Yanni complains that the weather was bad and agrees in a way with Phil he is quite obviously the confused friend of Phil. Shaun seems to believe that the day was completly good, he is obviously the beans of the group.

Very soon Phil decided that bed would be the best place for him at that moment. Yanni follows soon afterward, leaving Shaun to sit by himself. He broods over the day. Something had been not quite right about it. Something rang untrue in his mind. Suddenly his brain began to work and it clicked into place. He remembered seeing a man whatching him and his group. He now found it to be strange, as the man had no walking equipment and he was not dressedd for walking. He had looked like a tramp but he wondred what a tramp would be doing 50 miles from civilization.

But he could find no reason or explanation as to who or what the man was doing, so he dismissed him as no more than a tramp.

Shaun read the paper from cover to cover, taking in nearly all sporting stories and important headlines.

closed the door. The clock in the hallway chimed Nine o'clock. He sighed and started up the stairs, then as if by some force he stopped. Turning he remembered something about the tramp. No tramp he had ever seen wore an expennsive tweed jacket and had his hair cropped close. He bounded down the few stairs he had ascended and threw the living room door open. The lights went on and he grabbed the paper. The picture of the man on the front was that of the man he had seen by the old shed.

Phil led the way across the feild toward the old shed, as they neared it a growl could be heard from inside. Yanni who's one great talent in life was getting on with animals opened the door. The small dog bounded out barking and tearing viscously at Shauns trousers. Yanni talked to the dog and soon calmed it down as Phil entered the shed he came out a few seconds later "Nothing, he's gone" at that moment the dog and Yanni let out a bark of discovery. Phil and Shaun ran over. Yanni had picked up the wallet and began burrowing inside it, he pulled out a card giving a name and address. As Phil went back over the newspaper report a thought struck him, if this Scientist was the director of a Chemical Co. why was it not mentioned in the article. And why had the fact he was married been ommited.

"We must search for him," said Phil "he could die in this weather"

"We'll never find him" replied Shuan, "he could be anywhere by now, probably caught a lift at the main road."

"Maybe but why would he leave his dog behind?" argued Yanni.

"How do we know its his dog" Said Phil.

The front of the paper heralded the fact that the "great Chemical Scientist of the eighties goes missing."

Only a few hundred yards away the man has covered ten miles between house and hut very quickly. He moved silently and quickly away from the long shadow cast by the houses lighting.

Shaun had decided to go to bed he washed his plates and switched off the downstairs light, but just as he began to climb the stairs a thought struck him, does a tramp have short hair in a style, and a clean shaven tramp is virtually unheard of. He bounded down the few stairs he had climbed and burst into the living room. He snatched up the paper.

Two hours later Phil led the way across the field toward the hut, it had taken a long time to convince Phil and even longer to get on their wet clammy gear. Phil opened the door with a quik jerk. A furry ball burst out snorting and biting, it took hold of Shaun's leg and sunk its teeth into his wet suit. Shaun hopped around and tried to kick the dog off. Yanni stepped in and began calmly to talk to the dog, it responded.

Phil entered the hut, he re-appeared a few seconds later bringing the news that the man had gone out. They began to search the area for signs of the man. It was not long before a bark rang out in the now clear night sky. Phil and Shaun ran over towards the noise. Yanni was stooped over something with a torch, burrowing into it. He pulled out a card and read it "its the Scientist" he cried "Its him."

"We must search for him" said Phil "If he is wet he could die off pneumonia."

It was then that each one of them

"Its in the picture by the pool," said Shuan.

"But I agree with Phil we must look for him" voiced Yanni.

The gear they needed was grabbed together quickly. And soon they set out on their search. They went back to the Shed and circled it, just in case he had tripped and knocked himself unconcious they then followed the river up to the waterfall and down past the hut till the river dissappeared under the ground.

They began to despair of ever finding the missing man. That was until Shuan had a thought, he said "if you take the position the wallet to the shed it suggests he was heading for the main road."

When they reached the main road they found it was not very busy. They scoured everside the road for a couple of hundred metres, then a shout went up from Shuan. Yanni and Phil arrived quickly. The man lay on the ground with blood coming from his mouth his mouth in a track [?]. His eyes were open but they showed no expression, he was obviously very seriously injured. The dog licked its masters face but it made not a difference. Phil bent down to feel the mans pulse. Yanni put a cushion behind his head and leaned on Phil, feeling totally uncertain of how to help. His fear and concern plain to see. Shuans first reaction was to begin running to get help. The vivid picture of the three characters doing their own reaction could have been framed.

Within 30 minutes Shuan arrived back with the ambulance, but they were too late, the arm of the Scientist outstretched had a finality about it.

Next day the headline of the paper read "Brilliant Scientist kills

realized how cold they were.

"We'll never find him he's probably caught a lift at the main road by now" said Shaun.

"You're right" replied Phil.

"I am?" said Shaun in a tone of surprise "Why?"

"He'll be trying to get a lift."

The cars moved along the road at a tremendous speed, the lights glaring and bright, the road had dryed so the cars only noise is the engine and the wind howling as it whooshes past. They began to scour either side of the road for up to an hour until they found the man, it was Shaun who stumbled over him. He picked himself up and shouted to his friends, they arrived quikly. The man's face was a deathly pale, his ashen contoured cheeks stood out against his cheekbones. His eyes were black and somehow expressionless. The dog whimpered and licked the man's face the face did not alter its mask of death.

Phil bent to feel the mans pulse. Yanni stood one hand on Phil and the other on the ground by the man, he was obviously totally unsure of how to help. Shaun belted off to get help. The scene was vivid and frightening with the car lights flashing by and the cool night wind howling in the trees.

Only 20 minutes had gone by when Shaun returned with a passer by who happened to be a doctor. But as they reached the body Phil stood up. The man's mouth had a small trickle of blood winding its way accross his cheek. His arm outstretched carried a finality with it.

The inquest returned an open verdict, it could have been a suicide, his secret company had gone bust or he was killed because he had a business that was illegal, nobody would ever know.

himself" underneath was the story that told how his wife had left him and his secret company had gone bust. The comment by his wife summed the incident up, "he was too uncertain to be so clever" Yanni looked at this comment for a while and arrived at the fact he was better off than the scientist.

How Should Teachers Respond to a Student's Revised Version?

I have presented the whole of Greg's original draft and of his revised version partly because I find it interesting to compare the two from start to finish, but chiefly because for a teacher-reader, particularly a teacher who will have to allot a grade if this story is to go into an examination folder, having more than one version raises several important issues.

Should the revision be evaluated as a revision with the first draft available for comparison? This would appear to be reasonable if we make the assumption that an edited draft is likely to be an improvement on the writer's "first go." But on what criteria do we decide what is "better"? Obviously the opportunity that the student has had to proofread his work may result in a more mechanically accurate version, and whether or not that is the case will be immediately apparent. Greg consistently spells Shaun correctly for instance in Draft 2 and often incorrectly in Draft 1.

But if we are looking for more fundamental changes which affect the meaning of the piece, on what criteria are we to base our assessment of each draft? I referred in Chapter 4 to Donald Murray's observation in *Learning by Teaching* that as teacher-readers we tend to judge our students' offerings as though they were genuine "literature," in the sense that our benchmark for deciding what grade to give, is the work of fully-fledged authors such as James Joyce or Doris Lessing, in spite of the indisputable fact that the student writer is without exception, considerably less skilled— and certainly less experienced.

This is not to suggest that student writers are incapable of becoming professional writers—novelists, poets, journalists, script writers, or whatever. Indeed I believe that many more young people could become writers of excellence if they were encouraged to pursue their own meanings through their writing in the ways that this book suggests. I agree completely with Britton, that we should regard the development of an ability to shape meaning (on page or screen), as a spectrum which includes—and celebrates, the brainstorms, drafts and final presentations of five-year-olds such as those quoted earlier in this chapter—and also the tentative efforts of fifteen- or fifty-year-olds!

The problem that besets older pupils and erodes their confidence, is the insistence of the education system that teachers should increasingly sit in judgment on their efforts *as though they were professionals*. Many teachers I know who have to grade the writings of fourteen- to eighteen-year-old students for examination purposes, recognize that they are in an invidious position. Were it not for the examination system, they would much prefer to abandon grades and concentrate on constructive comments which could help learner-writers to pursue a writing journey to a satisfactory conclusion—in the light of their previous efforts and current intentions.

However, given that the demands for graded "validation" are not going to disappear just yet, I suggest that it would be helpful as a teaching profession to make the following public acknowledgment:

- We recognize that our students are not fully-fledged professional writers.
- We recognize that they have far less time to spend on assignments than professional writers do.
- Our evaluation of their work therefore will be based on the improvements that we can detect in their writing *as it progressively takes shape*.

In other words, our benchmark for evaluating the worth of what our students produce, should be where *they* finished compared to where *they* started. In the UK this would be very much in line with the "think positive" approach that GCSE criteria are encouraging. An original draft should be assessed for its potential, and a revised draft for any changes that have helped to realize that potential. If the writing is moving towards a poem, as we saw with the "War" and the "Winter" pieces, there may be several drafts as the writer shapes and reshapes thoughts and feelings.

So how would I assess Greg's revision in the light of his first draft? Leaving aside any improvements in encoding and general presentation, what about the shaping of the story, has that changed at all? Already in his original draft, Greg was experimenting with quite a complex cutting technique, moving back and forth from the missing scientist to the three walkers throughout. It is essential however, that at least one of the walkers glimpses the scientist outside the hut in the opening sequence if the denoument later is to be convincing.

In Draft 1 no such opportunity is given. The walkers are "Elsewhere"—indeed "a few miles off" and the scientist is only "getting ready to go out" of the hut. When I talked to Greg after he had written his first draft, I said that as a reader, I found this confusing and unsatisfactory but we did not discuss how the problem might be resolved. In Draft 2 Greg makes it clear by a couple of alterations which show how the man could have been spotted—he leaves the hut "to relieve himself" and the walkers pass "not more than 50 yards away." There is still no specific reference to the fact that Shaun sees him but we don't need to be told, the inference has been made.

Again in Draft 2 at the point where the man passes close to the house in which the three friends are staying, Greg lets us know that he has covered "ten miles between house and hut" on his way to the main road. Consequently the trek back to the hut in their "wet clammy gear" becomes a two-hour time-consuming penance. There is also the heightened sense of irony that precious time is being wasted moving away from the scientist, not towards him. In Draft 1 the relationship of the house to the hut is never made clear. Because these important topographical details are clarified in Draft 2 the story becomes more convincing.

The characters of the three friends (based I discovered on Greg and two of his pals) remain much the same in each version—but consistently so: Phil, the determined leader; Yanni, unconfident and willing to be led; Shaun, energetic and exhuberant with the wit to put two and two together and discover that it doesn't add up.

In both versions Greg gives the reader immediate clues about the "tramp" which suggest strongly that he is not what he seems. In his second version Greg has cut out the misleading impression that we are given (twice) in the original that the mysterious man is "contented." The other clues, which deliberately strike a discordant note are retained: his cropped hair and his cleanliness. Also of course, the dog, as the dog is the necessary finder of his master's wallet later in the tale.

Several visual images have been added to Draft 2: the dog's tongue "lolls around his open mouth," the orange waterproofs worn by the walkers are "darkened in patches" where the rain has soaked through, the cushion of the chair by the bookshelves is "indented with the shape of someone's back." In the second version the writer remembers to remind the reader of the stormy weather conditions throughout the narrative; he also draws together more compactly the part these conditions play in the action.

The syntax is still rather awkward in places but we have to remember that Greg is an emergent, not a professional story teller, making many decisions about reshaping in his edited version but with rough patches still in evidence among the smoother flow. The discovery of the wallet and subsequently of the man is achieved in three paragraphs in Draft 2, and the concluding paragraph is more succinct than Draft 1's ending.

The actual mechanics of each version are much the same. Greg's handwriting uses capital C's and S's throughout; he consistently misspells "quickly" and "quietly," "piece" and "field"; by and large however his spelling is accurate. He also uses speech marks, apostrophes and question marks, in both first and second drafts, though not 100% consistently.

It is the much clearer reshaping of the narrative that undeniably makes Draft 2 or *Mystery on the Moors* as Greg now calls it, a better version of *What Happened to Him?* Greg didn't have the formidable task of inventing landscape, characters and plot second time around. Rather he was able to reflect on all three strands as they already appeared on the page, reweaving them into a clearer pattern as he moved through the draft.

Let me stick my neck out and say that if the criteria for a GSCE grade were based on the potential of the first draft along with the improvements made in the revision, I would be happy to give Greg an A as a learner-writer, for what he attempted in the first place and worked at in his redraft, in spite of the mechanical inaccuracies which still remain.

There is also of course the question of the time required for close reflection by the teacher-responder. Undoubtedly it takes considerably longer to pay attention to editorial changes which affect the meaning than it does to make a quick scan for evidence of mechanical accuracy. But if shaping meaning is the prime objective, and the teacher's role that of constructive responder to the pupil's original draft and reflective responder to the final version, I cannot see that professionally, there can be any doubt that a thoughtful response to the meaning is more helpful than a "marking" of mistakes. As educators, the choice is clear. We have to work out ways in which we can offer more than merely proofreading to our pupils—at fifteen just as importantly as at five.

Developing a Point of View

In the opening chapter of this book I suggest that those who take a skill-based approach to education tend to assume that if the student is taught the rules for handling a particular medium correctly, when she comes to make sense with it, all will become clear. When writing is the medium in question, this assumption focuses attention on form. I remember the Head of History at my last school asking me to ensure that the English Department undertook to teach every 5th-year student how to write an essay, as though somehow, somewhere, a Platonic form existed which would transform uncertainty and confusion into elegant clarity. There is of course no magical mold which can produce an acceptable shape for whatever meaning is poured into it.

Young people need to experiment with *how* to express their thoughts while simultaneously discovering *what* those thoughts are. The shape their thoughts take will become clearer as they work out what they are clear about. Nor should we always hope for complete clarification as an outcome of continuing reflection. Where the issues are complex, if a student moves from stereotypic thinking to uncertainty, perhaps we should welcome that as a genuine advance!

In the last writing journey in this chapter, a fifteen-year-old student, Clare, is developing her own ideas about capital punishment—along with her sense of how to express them. Initially the teacher had asked everyone in the class to jot down in their journals what characterized a "good" argument essay. Clare wrote:

You have to have both points of view. The advantages, plus points for what you are arguing about. Disadvantages, negative points for what you are arguing about.

Also something interesting about what you are arguing about.

Why do we have the thing we are arguing about (the aims of them)— Is there any alternative we could do.

Clare then brainstormed in her journal the list of topics she might choose to argue about:

1. **Why do we have nuclear bombs.**
2. **Famine in other countries.**
3. **Croprol punishment.**
4. **Experiments on animals.**
5. **Should teachers strick.**

She then noted in her journal that for homework she would "write an outline" for numbers 4 and 5.

In effect, what Clare wrote next, was another think-write about a topic which had not been included on this list at all!

Clare's think-write for homework:

Death penalty people might think twice. People are put away for life they may as well die.

Capital punishment—I want to write whether or not it should come back. Whats good about it and whats not. Who should have capital punishment, whether the crime is bad enough. People who have been put away for murder are all cosy in prison when families and friends of the murdered are worried. The taxes for them are beginning [being?] payed and they eat the food why should they be supported when they kill people. But even though they have murdered I would find it hard to send someone to their death. I watch a film and a man was going to the gas chamber. We saw all the beginning in his cell the walking [?] the cell, shivering sweating, then into the chair and the scream as the gas fill the glass cage. It was horrible even though it was an act I can imagine it to be that way. It must be very hard to face death. I do not think they should be hung or gassed or shot. None of this perading up and down to be killed. A simple injection which will put them to sleep and never let them wake. I think this should be done to someone who has no purpose for murder does someone harm for no purpose. Like rape, some people murder once by accident they should not have capital punishment. But people [who] just murder, rape etc. should be capitally punished.

Whether Clare really had capital punishment in mind when she wrote down "croprol punishment," or whether she happened to see the condemned cell television program that evening—or whether her Dad asked her what she had for homework and then sounded off about the cushy life that murderers lead in prison, who is to say. What is clear, is that once she has decided on her topic, Clare begins recollecting what she knows and what she thinks, in order to be able to reconstruct her present views about capital punishment for her "argument essay."

Next Clare wrote a brief outline plus an additional thought or two which had not previously occurred to her:

Should we have capital punishment?
Crime after crime hapeneds through out the country and prisons fill up.
Honest people have to pay for their food out of their own hard earnt money
Why should this be?
Who should get capital punishment.
Film I watched. Man being put in a gases chamber.
—Just a simple injection to kill.
—Argue the points for and against.

It must be very hard to face death, even when you have comitted it yourself. To know you are going to die in a matter of hours. I think even the toughest criminals must understand what they put their victim through. I know I could never sentence someone to death I would always be thinking what happens if he is innocent?

Clare's first continuous draft for her essay now follows, written on three left hand pages of her notebook to leave space for her comments or "commentary" on what she has written so far on the right hand pages.

First draft: *Capital Punishment*

Crime after crime happens throughout the country and prisons fill. Honest people have to pay their taxes which feed, house and clothes these people. Why should murder[er]s not go through what they have put other people through? But then its not just murder[er]s but rapists and child molester[s]. I think capital punishment should come back but only in very exception cases e.g. "The Yorkshire Riper. This man just went out and sexual assorted women and also killed some. I think it was about 15 women. This man was put away for life but I think he should have been executed. Should it just be murders. But then rapist get away and they have probably put there victims through somethink which is worse than murder. But if you did execute someone for killing (murdering) wouldn't you be as bad as that person. There is all these sayings "two wrongs don't make a right" and "turn the other cheek." But then again you could say "an eye for an eye" etc it goes on. So what is right?

I once watched a film, at the end a man was going to be executed by the gase chamber. We saw this man an hour before he was about to go in to it. It was horrible, I felt sorry for him. No matter what he did, it did not seem right to put him through it. To know you are about to die a horrible death in a matter of minutes frighten(s) me. I have

Comments

I'm happy with my idea, I want to find information etc. on it. But I don't think what I have done so far is that good, it needs a lot of work on (it). What I did last night was sit down and use as much as I could still using my outline. I still need a good title. But I am hoping that it will come to me later on. Maybe when I am doing some res[ea]rch. I think I have got down what I am trying to put over. But I found it very hard to put into writing. It does need a lot of tid[y]ing up etc. I need to find information out, I will do that over the weekend. I'm not sure if I am for capital punishment or not as I said in one way I think it should come back in exception[al] casings. I think I must put my point over more clearly, I don't think it really flows yet. But hopefully it will in the next draft. I do need a conclusion, my one at the moment is that I would not send someone to death. I think I will have to change that. Maybe with what I would do. Information I will find will be the last person put to death why he or she was. Why it was stop and stuff like that (evidance to put in). I think the essay reads alright just needs some more good interesting information added.

always wondered what must go through your mind. Maybe this is pain enough for someone. They will probably understand what they put their victims through.

If there was ever capital punishment brought back, I don't think there should be hanging or gase chambers. I mean to be made to sit down and locked in a chair and watch the glass case fill with poisonous gas makes me shiver. I think the worsed capital punishment must be the electric chair. You can always imagine that the first bolt wont kill you so the[y] do it again. The easest way would be an inject which would put you to sleep or a tablet. Or maybe in there sleep when there not expecting it, you could put in some gas through a vent which would never let them wake up. I don't feel they should be told what day they are going to die.

Clare then produced a second outline, which includes some of the facts that she has now researched:

Comments

By 1965 the only offences which were punished by death were certain kinds of murder, the burning of dockyards, ships arsenals and high treason etc

Crime after crime happens throughout the country and prisons fill up. In the eighteenth century 200 offences were punished by one death penalty, most were very unimportant crimes.

—write about evidance information etc.
—Argue whether it should come back
—Film I watched
—If it did come back what should be used
—The end about where to draw a line.

Nowadays there is so many terrable crimes which you hear on the TV and read in the paper about rapists, molesters, terrible murders and people who torcher there victims, it would be very hard to say who should get the death penalty. The problem is, w(h)ere do you draw the line...?

In her final draft which she calls "Do Two Wrongs Make a Right?" Clare *still* can't decide her three key issues: whether capital punishment should be brought back, if so how it should be administered—and for whom. I must say that I have sympathy with her in her dilemma; I would not want to penalize her as a writer for keeping an open mind. I am sure that the writing journey she made, free writing, drafting and commenting on each of her drafts helped her to clarify the issues, even if she couldn't arrive at solutions. In that sense it was a journey well worth making.

Final draft

Do Two Wrongs Make a Right?

Crime after crime happens throughout the country and prisons fill up. In the eighteenth century 200 offences were punished by the death penalty, most were very unimportant crimes. By 1965 the only offences in England to be punished by the death penalty were certain kinds of murder, the burning of dockyards, ships, arsenals and high treason.

The kinds of murder punished by death were murders done while committing a theft, murder by shooting; murder done while resisting arrest or trying to escape, the murder of a police officer or prison officer doing his duty. The death penaly in Britain was carried out by hanging. Many people wished to abolish capital punishment completely. They said that a human life is sacred and that it has a bad effect on human beings to execute their fellowmen. They were saying "Two wrongs don't make a right" and "Turn the other cheek." But in this day and age I feel it should be "an eye for an eye." Why should murderers get away with murder? They should be put through what they have put other people through.

If capital punishment was brought back it would save money for the government, they would not have to house so many prisoners, supply so much food and so many clothes. But then it is a human life you are talking about so does that all matter?

I once watched a film, at the end a man was sent to the electric chair. Even though this man was only acting you could still imagine what it was like. In his cell, waiting just waiting for the last couple of minutes of his life to pass. After killing someone you must think that you are going to go to hell. I think the worst bit must be sitting in the chair, tied down just waiting for that bolt of electricity to go through your body and kill you. I will always wonder what is going through their heads. One thing is they will know what they have put their victims through. But to know you are going to die there and then is horrible. I would find it hard to put the cruellest murder(er) through that.

If capital punishment was brought back then I don't think we should use the electrice, hanging or gas chamber but a simple injection which will put you to sleep or when you are asleep one night and without you knowing it some sort of gas fills your room and you never wake up in the morning.

I don't feel they should be told what is going to happen to them, just that one day in the next week or so they are going to die, it should just be done unexpectedly. In America they have death row. Men just waiting to die. If maybe it did come back to England then I don't think there should be a waiting list.

I approve of capital punishment in exceptional cases. I think people who murder for there own gain should be executed. But you could also put rapists and molesters under that. So were do you draw the line?

Moving Towards a Finished Product: A Final Reflection

Poems, stories, autobiographical descriptions, personal opinions—most of these writings which move towards a finished piece or product also move towards that end of the spectrum of writing that Britton defined as "poetic," more commonly defined as "literary." Why as young people develop their ability to shape meaning through writing, are nonliterary pieces so rare by comparison? I find the question an intriguing one and can only speculate on possible reasons at the conclusion of this chapter.

Perhaps it has something to do with the distinction that I drew in my opening chapter between reconstructing and re-creating. When youngsters at the age of five or indeed fifteen draw upon their own firsthand experiences, these have already been sufficiently assimilated to provide a wealth of material which they can tap, and which perhaps is drawn more readily to mind than the more disjointed secondhand information that as learners they are still struggling to come to grips with. They have ownership of their direct encounters with the world which can be transformed into poems and stories or more directly autobiographical pieces with some confidence—if they are given adequate time and encouragement to recollect, re-create and re-present. Personal opinions are more difficult to transform with the same coherence if they are based—as many of our opinions inevitably are, on secondhand rather than firsthand experience. Clare has never committed a criminal act nor has she had any opportunity to talk to someone who has. Consequently her meaning-shaping is bound to be more tentative. In this respect an "argument essay" poses the same difficulties as any other "reconstructive" writing insofar as it is bound to be based on the inexperience of the young writer.

There is another difficulty about producing nonliterary finished products. Pupils are presented with far fewer examples of such writing in school, unless we take into account school textbooks—and who would expect any pupil to produce one of those! Most primary and secondary pupils hear at least some poems and stories read aloud during the course of their school careers but how many nonliterary pieces of writing do they hear? The occasional article from a newspaper perhaps. Therefore they have little (if any) opportunity to absorb how experienced writers actually write—about mathematics, or history or geography, etc., except in textbooks!

I guess the same problem—how to produce coherent nonliterary finished products confronts students in universities as well as pupils in schools.

Perhaps for all learners it is unreasonable to expect "finished" writing of this kind.

In the next chapter, I consider writing which is not aiming to turn itself into a finished piece, where the main function of the "thinking made visible" is to help the writer make sense of her uncertainties—sometimes of a personal nature but largely in the field of new information. It is my view that more "process oriented" writing of this kind would be helpful across the curriculum, to learners of all ages from primary school children to doctoral students.

7

Making Sense—in Journals,
Learning Logs, Think-Books

A Glance Backwards: 1968–88

When James Britton and the London Institute team collected their extensive sample of pupil writings across the curriculum from the 1st, 3rd, 5th, and 7th years of secondary schooling in the late sixties (see *The Development of Writing Abilities 11–18*), the vast bulk of that sample turned out to be writing to "give evidence." Writing was unquestionably regarded as a mode of expression chiefly to indicate what had been learned, not as one to learn *through*. Even in English, most of the writing was about other people's writing, largely recorded knowledge *about* a text or an author. There were very few examples indeed of pupils using writing itself as a learning process—writing to help them to think, writing to come up with questions, writing to reflect about the work they were doing in science or history or maths or English—writing to map their own progress and to share their thoughts and feelings as learners with their teachers.

I knew a few teachers who were already experimenting in the mid-sixties with writing diaries or learning logs, in an effort to broaden the scope for writing in the classroom, seeking at the same time to offer themselves to their pupils as "partners in a learning dialogue," to use the London Institute team's term. Ten years later in the mid-seventies I came across the Bay Area Writing Project and the teachers who wrote their own journals throughout the month-long Summer Institute—and continued to write reflectively for themselves long after that intensive four weeks of writing together had come to an end.

At that time I also discovered Gabriel Jacob's account of how he had patiently, and slowly but successfully, encouraged his nine- to eleven-year-olds to keep think-books in which they wrote to make their thinking visible—both for themselves and for their teacher. Jacob's main aim was to develop every child's confidence in her own capacity to think, and to encourage his pupils to value whatever thoughts came to them, lateral or logical, inside the classroom or out. Jacobs was seeking to convince his kids that writing was a powerful thinking agent, not the straitjacket to thought that it can so woefully become.

For the past decade a growing number of primary and secondary teachers in my own county have been creating a variety of opportunities for pupils to "think onto paper" for a variety of purposes, and it is chiefly from their classrooms that I shall draw my examples. The project that we have run jointly for the past three years with our neighboring county, Somerset, is called *Write to Learn,* christened from Donald Murray's book of that title, which was published around the time our project started. As members of the National Writing Projects both in the UK and the USA, we know—and are reassured by the knowledge, that an increasing number of teachers in both our countries are enthusiastically using journals, learning logs or think-books with pupils of all ages.

And yet . . . and yet . . . Before the picture takes on too rosy a hue, let me also express some doubts as to the extent to which students are now writing to learn. I still see many assigned one-off pieces of writing at both primary and secondary levels which ignore the learner's need to make sense. In fact as I mentioned in a previous chapter, one-off writing corrected by the teacher mainly for mechanical errors, is commonplace. I have also no doubt that if another national sample of writing in schools were to be taken now, twenty years on from the London Institute's Survey, the bulk of it would still be "evidential"—writing to communicate what was known rather than writing to reflect on what was being learned.

However, I would hope that think-writing of one kind or another would show up more distinctly on the map of current practice (as would drafting and redrafting), in a way that was only microscopically visible in most schools for most children in the fifties and sixties. I offer this word of caution though, at the commencement of this chapter, because I believe that we still have much to learn about how to introduce—and how to encourage, the developing use of learning logs, journals or think-books in ways that will help pupils to make sense of new information and unfamiliar concepts.

Only the other day a teacher voiced the anxiety in one of our *Write to Learn* groups, that pupils would become tired of, and thus would shrug off "think-writing" much as they shrugged off and hastened through their one-off assignments. We need to continue sharing ideas and working together to ensure that this reduction to a mere school requirement doesn't happen. I don't believe that it will, once a pupil (whatever her age), has experienced the power that writing possesses, to help her to sort out her ideas. If however we cannot find fresh ways to help our students take hold of writing as a powerful mental act, it is in danger of remaining at best a dreary task and at worst a dreaded chore. I am writing this chapter fully aware therefore that there is still much to be learned and that I am one of the learners.

What's in a Name?

One of the confusions that sometimes makes discussion difficult, is a confusion about terms—what some refer to as think-books, others refer to as journals or as learning logs; under any of these names pupils may be writing to express their feelings, to sort out their ideas or to ask questions about their work. Some regard journals as essentially sacrosanct to the writer and only to be shared (even with the teacher), if the writer so wishes; others regard them as a useful basis for small group and possibly class discussion—others again as a useful form of self-assessment and personal profiling.

These variations on how we use different names or different functions for reflective "process" writing are unimportant—as long as our pupils are clear what our expectations are—and in discussion with colleagues, as long as we make clear to each other those same expectations.

In the rest of this chapter I shall seek to exemplify the functions for logs, journals or think-books as I have come across them, with appropriate entries from primary and secondary pupils to illustrate this range of purposes. I'm interested to note that I have just used the word "entries"; perhaps this is as good a way as any of distinguishing "writing to learn" from "writing to make." The latter moves through stages of development with a sense of direction towards a goal: the finished product. The former has no such terminus in mind. A journal, log or think-book entry can be as short or as long and rambling as the writer likes. She can skip from thought to thought or she can reflect on one idea as it circles around and around. She can ask questions without having to answer them and express feelings without having to justify. The point is, because the thinking is written, it is visible—and is therefore available for further reflection—by the writer, and in many instances by the teacher as an interested party in the whole business of learning.

Personal Think-Books

This first collection of entries comes from a class of eight-to eleven-year-olds in a village primary school. Several years ago the head of the school read Jacobs' account of how he had encouraged his children to "write to think" and he has been encouraging his pupils to keep think-books ever since. It will be clear from the entries that I quote here—with the children's permission, that they have been written for "Mr B" as a trusted and respected "reader" without whom their inner "puzzlings over" would never have been formulated. Most of their entries are questions addressed directly to him.

Asking Questions

Jane (8)

Mr B I am very puzzeled about a problem witch is right. God made the Earth or The Earth never started? This problem has been running

round my mind for some time. But since I have not had my think book I could not write to you. Also I would like to know how God made the Earth?

How is water made? How do you make sand? I know rocks were mud but how do you make mud become rock? How do you put life into animals? how were songs made by birds? Also I would like to know how Swindon Songsters thought up their name I would like to know. I have no idea how they thought up the Songsters bit.

Right Jane. Mud can become rock when it is covered with lots of other rocks and mud and compressed. Also if it is made hot it will turn into rock—think of pottery and kilns.

Now, as far as God and the Swindon Songsters are concerned, I'd like you to do some more of your excellent thinking.

Sandra (8)

Mr B I wonder how God made the world so quick because he made the world in seven days. I have been wondering how God made the world over the holiday. How did God make all of the people in the world? Why dont men have babies? When was the first person in the world born? What was the first animal in the world to be made. Would it take about two days for somone to write a whole book.

Great thinking Sandra. Please come and talk to me.

Andy (8)

Mr B I would like to know how compewters work I think the compewter chip oparats (the) compewter but I don't know how the chip works I thing in the chip there is a power sause which has wirers oparating diffrent parts. I would also like to know how keys Work I think from the chip a wire leeds to a shokit that gose on to the monata and then it gose to a nother chip and it prints it out what do you think Mr B

I think you might know more than I do Andy. Come and talk please.

Tess (10)

Mr B, Suppose your Mum and dad got divorced and they had some children one of them was a daughter and she found this nice sort of chap and they fell in love and got married and then her mum fell in love with the boys dad what would happen because well you arent aloud to marry step sisters or brothers? I think the mum would have to find another man because the daughter got there first didn't she?

What's all this about Tess? Actually I think the Mum could marry her daughter's father-in-law.

I read it in a comic but I didn't see the end and I didn't think the mum could get married to the boys dad.

Margaret (8)

Dear Mr B,

Are vampires really real and living on earth. Because I think that they are not real and that they are not really living on this earth. And why do we have to ask our mums if someone can stay the night is it because our mums do not want us to make a mess in the house because he mums do not like tidying up the mess that we have made with our freinds and Mr B why can men not have baby's is it because God thought that there would be to many babies in the world.

This is very good thinking Margaret. You are quite right about vampires and mums. Men cannot have babies because their bodies are not made in the same way as women's. All creatures need males and females to make babies and it's always the females who have the babies. It's been like that for millions of years. Tell me if you are still puzzled.

Dear Mr B, I am not puzzled any more. Mr B why do dogs have fur and people do not is it because dogs stay outside more of the time and Mr B why do we have birthdays is it to selibrate when we were born and Mr B why do cats have pointed ears and dogs and other animals and Mr B why do elephants have long noses is it because they like eating tree leaves of(f) tree so they have to reach up to the leaves and Mr B why do skunkes every time they lift up their tail let of a smell is it to protect them selfs.

Mike (11)

Mr B will it be posidle to put a plug on one end of a lead and put a plug on the outher end and plug it into a plug socket and put the outher end ina dobble socet plug (with out ent power) and swich it on and in the dobble socket put a plug so that it will work wot ever you put in the dobble soet.

Draw a plan of this on the next page and then I'll tell you what I think, please.

Mike then drew a diagram which is no longer available and his teacher wrote:

Don't try this it could be fatal!

Sharing Your Feelings

Miriam (9)

Mr B - Soon my mum will be going into hospital and I am very worried I think I will have to help evon more than I do but the only thing is that I go and help antey J and when I get back it is about half past five.

If you do your best that's all that anybody can expect. You can't do everything.

Deb (10)

Mr B—Did my book frighten you in places?? My mum and dad are splitting up maybe because mummy is fed up with daddy and daddy is getting very nasty with mummy by saying all sorts of horrible things and making mummy cry, things which aren't even true please don't tell anyone because it might not even happen yet.

My Mum was always threatening to leave my Dad but she never did. I know it's worrying but it's very early days yet, Deb. What do you do when they are arguing?

Topical Thinking

Joanne (11)

I was listening to the radio when I heard that people say that insted of mrs thacher giving money to other countrys she should give it to our country. I think it should be split in half so some of our country gest some and some other contrys get some. or Bob Geldof should make a record for this country to raise mouny like for the great allman street Hospital. What do you think?

I think Mrs Thatcher should find more money for Great Ormond Street Hospital by spending less on weapons.

Jo (10)

Dear Mr B, I think the British treated the aborigines really bad when they first came to Australia. They saw them as savages and hunted them like animals. I think that was really bad. I don't know why the ozes are celabrating only two hundred years it should be the aborigines that are celabrateing because they have been in Australia for four hundred years and it beats us with our little two hundred years by a long way. So the aborigines really do diserv the party.

Yes, I think you are right Jo—it wouldn't have been quite so bad if the aborigines feelings about the celebrations had been taken note of. It's almost as if they had been ignored.

The Teacher's Role

Several points strike me about these think-book entries:

1. Mr B is patently a trusted teacher. The children can ask whatever questions they like, express their immediate concerns, reflect on what is happening in the world around them.
2. He is their trusted reader, principally to take note of whatever is on their minds. Many of their questions are, in a sense, unanswerable— and to attempt to answer them at all specifically would be impossible. They are *thoughtful* questions, to be registered and acknowledged, not slot machine questions which demand a ring-a-ding answer.
3. Without the opportunity offered by the pupils' think-books, these questions and concerns could never have been formulated yet no "National Curriculum" could put these pupils' questions on its agenda. However, too compulsive a concern with specific "programs of study" could endanger the existence of think-books which not only acknowledge but actually encourage the unpredictable and emphasize the validity of individual thoughts and feelings.

Stephen's Thinking Book

In another school "thinking books" is what Stephen's top junior class called the four-by-four-inch booklets which their teacher gave to them to write "whatever they liked" for her. Here are Stephen's entries over half a term along with his teacher's responses:

I think that it will be Cahos when we move in everything is in packing cases or a box of somesort. Im still wondering what to do for my birthday. I also think that Bob Russels is a rip-off. I think my girlfriend still loves me.

I shall be interested to hear more about the moving chaos when it happens! What is Bob Russels?

Bob Russels is a army surplus store and he sells things like, para boots, combat trousers, webbing packs that sort of thing. Last weekend I packed up all my things in my room and got really fed up afterwards, I went and chose a video to watch it was called Police Acadamey and I think it is the best film in the world. I have a cold and mum thinks that if I carry on to sit to long in a bath after it has gone cold I will catch peamonea I don't belive her. I think James is lucky having dynamite pouches. I'am getting some combat trousers for christmas. I still haven't

decided what to do for my birthday. I think I want to be in the Royal marines or the RAF when I grow up. If I were in the RAF I would be a fighter pilot.

That's funny about the bath—it's just what my Mum used to say! I never caught pneumonia! I expect your room feels pretty bleak now—What made that video particularly good?

It was very funny and far feacthed.
My Granma has cancer, I am very upset. I found out last night when I herd my dad on the phone. We all ready have a cancer reashech box and any money I have I put in there. I hope she doesn't die.

There's not much I can say to help you to cope with this horrible news. You must think about the doctors and hope for their skill to help your grandmother.

I went ice scating at the Link Centre with Paul for my birthday I only went with Paul because he is the only one of my freinds who can ice scate. I think my new house is great! We live next to a very nice couple Margret one of the couple is a Authour I have had a look in the library but to no avail she writes under her maidon name Margret Bacon! perhaps you have one of her books?

My mother has had some of her books which I have read—I'll see if she has any children's books.

I think *My side of the mountain* is great! I think I might run away one day. I am not allowed to climb any trees in the garden I think this a great dissapointment. I think that sataurday morning squad training swiming is tortue you have to swim 2 hours non-stop as fast as you can!

How far do you get in 2 hours? It must build stamina! Where will you run to?

Well, if you consider—the warm up is 40 lengths or 800 metres you can gess how far we go, and that only takes 10 mins

FRUSTRAION!

Frustraion! is a thing that can get people all over the world angry. I get frustrated when I am trying to draw somthing and I can't, and then my brother anoys me and then I get crosser and crosser so I hit my brother and start a fight and then dad comes up and gets and angry and then mum burns what she is cooking because she is trying to keep us under control and then she gets Frustrated and starts a qurral with dad and then I say be quite I am trying to draw then my brother says shut up and we start a fight. . . . e.t.c. That is pure frustaion.

It makes me think of a circle going round and round and round.

I think I would run to coleshill or badbury clump.

I think I would be scared of there!

THE FATE OF JERMY VISICK

I think the fate of Jermy Visick is brillient I have got to the part were Matthew went down the mine a second time with Jermy. I don't blame Matthew for running away the first time I think I would have.

War!

The word war is a word that emidiatly sums it up in athour words it is a Ted Hughes word. A war is when the soliders who have been training all there career suddenly put it into use, the real thing.

Most of my freinds think that war is brillent and think having to kill another person is nothing, but I know how hard the army is even in this modern age. A miletery doctor once said that the 5 things to cure shell shock were a cup of strong tea and 4 sugurs. And tea is part of the vast problem of supplies in brittan now there are 2 regiments devoted to supplieing armys once they have invaded a country, As in Dunkurk as soon as they had invaded they needed, bullets and amunition, first aid, food, clothes and lots of other things and the only way they could do that was by the ingunutie of the sapper both for capturing the beachs and then building a masive ponntoon bridge to streach across the channel to get supllies across, and to the amaze ment of the soliders who didn't even know it exzisted. Ant do you remember the tank which had a frail fitted at the frount to explode mines on the beachs. and that famous war cry "Follow the Sapper" when the need to get foward was most urgent.

You may enjoy some of the books set in the war—Dolphin Crossing is about Dunkirk and very moving.

Wonder

I wonder why we were put on this earth and who made the earth and sometimes I wonder if I am dreaming and the whole world isn't true and I wonder why I am wondering about things and wonder about ev-erthing, the world is strange and that gives us cause to wonder. I wonder why I am writing this. It seems silly but I am wondering about wonder, wonder is strange like the world and the human race. I wonder what I'll get for christmas. and I often wonder what its like to be someone else and think what they think and know what they think about me. I often wonder if there are aleins out in space.

I wonder!

I'm interested in your wondering about if you are dreaming everything. I sometimes wonder that too—I am in your dream and you are in mine!

My Side of the Mountain

I Think *My Side of the Mountain* is brrilient, I think it is about how life is today and however much you try to escape it you can't. I think the way he was so inderpandant and he had (to) conquer modern life until people get to know about it, then it leaks out and more and more people know, and then he has to come back, but he didn't his Mum, dad and family came to him. I think that if he hadn't been discovered he would have gone back himself, because he couldn't do without the life he had been with for so long, and I think this applys to everone, however much courage or bravery you have you will never escape the life you have lead before.

To me—and I am sure to you, Stephen's thinking book makes possible an interesting glimpse into a whole range of ideas and feelings which may never otherwise have surfaced in a shareable way from this ten-year-old's head. I know that his teacher still values this small booklet as evidence of the trust with which he shared some of his innermost thoughts with her.

Kev's Dialogue with His Form Tutor

My last example of think-writing which is volunteered by the pupil in a conversational way, comes from what you might call an unlikely lad! It's probably the most Kev ever wrote about anything that year between twelve and thirteen, perhaps even for the rest of his school career—chiefly because he had a teacher who listened to what he wrote and was willing to respond to his thoughts without evaluating them:

Mister C you know I got that BMX of mine well I was out on last night and me and Brian Baxter got stopt by a copper and I must av got a puncher so I askt this copper whether hed put my bike in the car an he seid if it gos in my bote It stays thare, so I seid you can by it of mee for 200 quid and he seid it would be cheper to nik one.

I bet you didn't have any lights on your bike, did you?

No I din't, but Im plsst with my self becas last night on my BMX I jumt just over one meter high.

So, you're going to start drama again next term are you?

Yes it beter than doing english any way do you think that say me dave nige have a comp on BMX aganst other clasis or against ouselves.
Well Mr C if you can name wate form pieriod it going to be will get som ramps for triks or we cold even have a cors to rase.

As I've already said, if you want to do anything like that, get permission first and then work out your plans in detail. See Mr. W.

OK IL av a word with spud and Nigal and see whot thay wont to do.

Are you coming up to see the Snow Queen this week?

No! il shal be out on my BMX pratusin some stuns like arid tearns and lay downs.

What's a "lay down" (on B.M.X.s)?

a lay down or otherwis none as a table top, is wen you in mid air veracal with your bars twistid.

Have you seen Tony's BMX yet?

Yes I hav it's alright but I woden't get one. If you tearn your T.V. set on chanle four, on muday's 6 oclok you will se the BMX frosh's chapionships int's on four six weeks and it has all the star's on it.

I'm afraid I haven't got a telly. Has the BMX championship been good? What do they have to do to win?

Well at the begining of a race there's about 7 peopul or less and you wat for the lit's to turn Green or a man say's rider's redy pedals redy Go! and you go like a bat out of hell.

Do they just race or do you have to do stunts as well?

When you enter a compatishan you youshaly do one or anouther befor you start and you keep it like that, but thare is quite alot of plasis were you do both. by the Way how did you get on last night playing kriket.

We won at cricket thanks. I got 3 not out and Mr W and me scored the winning runs.
Good luck for next year, Kev! How do you feel about going to the Upper School?

Well done about the cricket, but I'm not sure about going up, I will probably like it when I get thare, but at the moment ?

Your fingers might have been itching there, to correct at least some of Kev's spelling errors—"there," not "thare"; "said" not "seid"—and so on. Similarly to comment on the sudden rash of apostrophes that breaks out towards the end! I felt the urge myself as I was typing it out. But I am convinced now that such itchings and urges must be resisted.

Each of these pupils has been *using* writing to think for him or herself—but primarily to share those thoughts with a trusted reader. They have all succeeded in becoming communicators, including Kev. They have all made the medium of written language work for that purpose—and if in so doing they have become a little more conversant with the code, good luck to them. It would have been quite inappropriate to foreground it as a writing issue however, in any of these conversations on paper.

Reading Logs for Reading Journeys

Specialist English teachers most commonly encourage students to use think-writing as a means of speculating about or interpreting a literary text. I have called this section "Reading Logs for Reading Journeys" because, just as shaping meaning into writing takes time, so does reaching an understanding of someone else's writing, whether a novel or short story, a poem or play. If the text is fairly lengthy, then the log can track the reader's thoughts as she makes her way through it—along with the changing reactions that she may possibly experience as the plot unfolds and the characters reveal themselves more fully. If the text is shorter and the meaning more densely compacted, the log can take the reader several times over the same ground, enabling different observations and insights to be made from each encounter.

Most importantly, because the log frees the writer-responder from the constraints of the formal essay, thoughts can flow freely and retain the voice of the writer honestly and openly. She knows that this is a record of her present reactions to the text, that these reactions may well change as the journey continues and that her teacher is not going to hold anything she says in evidence against her. This is not to say that the teacher will necessarily agree with her point of view. As a "partner in dialogue" he may respond by asking questions or calling attention to aspects of the text she may not have noticed yet. "Writing to learn" often leads to discussion which in turn can lead to further think-writing. The time given for writing may be brief—perhaps a ten-minute burst from everyone in the group, including the teacher, on their first encounter with a poem, so that everyone has some "initial impact" ideas to share in the small group discussion that follows; or maybe a longer portion of time after the class has watched a video or come to the end of a short story; or for as long or as little time as the student is prepared to give for a log-writing homework assignment.

As all teachers who keep logs with their students know, the ways in which we can think-write are many and various but every entry, however brief its span, helps the reader-writer to bring meaning to the text and to make meaning of it. As Diane Cookston wrote in *What's Going On?* students who keep reading logs also write better essays. They have noticed more on their journey through the text and can therefore tell more at the end of it.

The examples which follow come from a 3rd-year, 4th-year and 6th-year class at the same comprehensive school, taught by the same teacher who has clearly found a way of convincing her pupils that they can think for themselves. It was difficult to make a selection but I hope these entries give a flavor of the running commentaries that are otherwise only flickeringly and privately heard inside the heads of silent readers.

Thirteen- to Fourteen-Year-Olds' Responses to Roll of Thunder, Hear My Cry by Mildred Taylor

Speculating (Ian)

Chapter 1—As I got into this chapter the first (thing) that struck me was how much it was to them to own their own land and not to sharecrop on white mans land. For Cassies father had even gone hundreds of miles to work on the railroad, only seeing his family every now and then, just so they could keep their land.

Although the days of slavery are supposedly gone, life for the blacks was certainly very hard not just privilleges taken away from them but the scorn and humiliation dished out by the whites.

What I wonder at is how you bring up a family in the circumstances, how do you explain to them? How do you stop them trying to retaliate? How do you bring them up as good kids when there being treated like second class citizens? But thinking about it this whole book conjures up the thoughts How? and Why?

Reflective running commentary (Darren)

Chapter 7—At the start of Chapter seven Stacey has to face Mama and Hammer about giving T.J. his new coat. I think Mama and Hammer were a bit hard on Stacey. I don't like T.J. and think it would be very easy for T.J. to make someone give him something. The way T.J. treats Stacey, if I were to be Stacey I would not be so friendly or easy on him. If I were Hammer, I would go and get the coat from T.J. but I suppose that Stacey has to look after himself. Later on in the chapter Mr Jamison comes over to the Logan's, and offers to back the Logan's loan on the land. The Logan's didn't answer, but acknowledged the offer, I think Mr Jamison is a good friend, and thinks of the Wallaces the same as the Logan's do. In my opinion the Logans should accept Mr Jamison and his offer, but of course they know they have to be careful.

Focus on feeling (Sophie)

I know how the children felt when they were forced by their mother to wear a skin because it is similar to be forced to wear clothes and shoes by your parents and you will do almost anything to get rid of them.

Each day Little Man got more and more annoyed about the bus splashing him and when you read the book you could tell how frustrated he was getting and you could also tell that he was going to do something about it.

The children must have felt guilt as well as pleasure as they watched the bus diving into the enormous great ditch. When they later found out what might happen to them and their family they would probably have started to panic and want to know more about what the lynch mob and the clan clucks clan did to black people who didn't know their place.

Dramatic improvisation (Karen)

While they were reading this novel, the class were given another example of racist attitudes to black slaves in the form of a sermon given by a white preacher. This is how Karen chose to comment on it in her log:

The answer I would give to the Precher who gave the sermon if I was black or a slave

"Poor creatures you little consider when you are idle . . . when you steal and waste . . . when you are saucy and impudent . . . and will not do the work you are set about . . ."

Please refer to us as people or with something that has the same respect for I am sure you would not refer to yourself as a creature. We are never idle, only when you make us for we are not superhuman who can live any where and servive anything, when you whip us or thrash us we become ill, mental and physically and unable to work, like you would be if you were treated in the same way you treat us.

We only steal because you make us, but we never waste anything. What do we have to waste? It is you who wastes normally lives, the lives of slaves and black people. This is a far bigger crime than any of us are able to do

You say we are saucy and impudent, what do you mean by this? You say we will not do the work we are set about. Have you ever thought why this is?

"You do not consider the thoughts you are guilty of, towards your masters and mistresses are faults done against God himself who has set your masters and mistresses over you in his own stead and expects what you would do for them just as you would do for him . . ."

Have you ever considered your faults you are guilty of, I am sure yours are far greater than ours for it is you who treats humans like you. In a [?] way, [?] and horrid, and not like God would want you to do. This is why we do not always do as our Masters and Misstress want, for they are often wrong in our eyes of God. It is not us who needs Masters and Misstress but you.

"They are God's overseers and if you are faulty towards them, God himself will punish you severely in the next world. Unless you relent and strive to make amends by your faithfulness and diligence in time to come."

God himself should punish you and our masters and misstress severly in the next world, for it is you who needs to be, and I am sure he will. It is you who need to relent, you need to, we don't.

Fourteen- to Fifteen-Year-Olds' Initial Responses to Romeo and Juliet

Mulling it over (Ashleigh)

Romeo seems to be the type of person who likes dreaming romances. He is strange towards women. A few days age he was madly in love with Rosaline yet as soon as he saw Juliet he considered Ros. a crow. Did Romeo really love Ros? If not, why did he act as though he did? She can't have been that special.

Well, Juliet must be because after seeing her the night before, Romeo goes to the friar to arrange a secret marriage. The Friar is very shocked that Romeo doesn't care for Ros any more and even more shocked that R wants to marry a Capulet!

A response colored by previous experience (Debbie)

I think Shakespeare is a very talented writer but I personally do not like his work. At primary school we had our first encounter of his books. A small group of us were taken to a corner with a few books of "Romeo and Juliet." Together we worked at, talked about and read a large part of the book. I can now understand the humor and enjoyment it provoked in its day, but I do not find it funny or entertaining. Because of this encounter I do not ever want to see it again. I could not start to understand the story and I found the language impossible to cope with. During the time we studied it I found it hard to keep awake.

I think I was far too young to start reading this complex novel. Now that we have started this book again I find it very hard to concentrate on it. Even though Jane Eyre is not really my type of book I could at least take it away and read it by myself. Even now I would feel totally stuck if I had to read Romeo and Juliet by myself.

As a result of that unfortunately premature introduction to our greatest English writer, Debbie now approaches anything written by him with the same lack of confidence in her own capacity to make sense, that I approach crossword puzzles. To her the Bard seems equally cryptic! Neil on the other hand has no such qualms:

Challenging the text (Neil)

I think that it is a bit odd that Romeo and Juliet are in each others arms and saying that their lives are not worth living without each other after they only met each other for the first time a few minutes ago.

After Romeo is discovered gatecrashing Capulet's party why is he not thrown out immediately? Instead he is allowed to stay and chat up Capulet's only daughter. What happens to Paris who was supposed to be introduced to Juliet? Surely Lady Capulet whose idea it was in the first place would make more of an effort.

I can't help thinking that if there was no Tybalt the relations between the Montague and Capulet families would be a great deal better. Also Tybalt's powers of perception must be truly brilliant to recognize a Montague underneath a mask just by his voice. Also another great disappearance—what happened to Rosaline? Did she find true love elsewhere? Up until Act 2 Scene 2 the Nurse was the most prominent character. The nurse is a very good character to have around as she tends to throw a little more light on the more complicated situations.

I think that the more prologues the better, it is a very good idea to have one at the start of each act.

Going on to Act 2 now, I think Benvolio and Mercutio seem a little bit too concerned for Romeo's safety than is normal. I mean why do they follow Romeo around all day trying to persuade him not to see Juliet? Would it not be easier and a lot less dangerous for Romeo and Juliet to meet on neutral ground.

I am surprised that the nurse did not suggest a more sensible and safe wedding. How can Romeo and Juliet possibly lead a normal married life? They will be lucky if they set eyes on each other once a day let alone speak to each other.

Surely the answer to their problem would be to elope together. This seems to be the only thing that will keep them together now as Romeo has just killed Tybalt and got himself banished from Verona.

Sixteen- to Seventeen-Year-Olds' Responses to The Rainbow

This advanced-level English Literature group had been encouraged by their teacher to read *Sons and Lovers* as preparatory reading for their study of *The Rainbow* as one of their set texts. They had also looked at photocopies of some of D. H. Lawrence's letters to Frieda and talked together about the biographical background to both novels.

The two reading logs from which I quote seem to me to be written chiefly for these students to conduct their own personal dialogues—between their inner ear and their thoughts as they arrive, through the writing, on the page. The move from writing for your teacher to writing for yourself is in my view a sophisticated one which takes time and practice.

Jemma's thoughts on the opening chapters

This is definitly Lawrence! Reading even the first few sentences fills me with warmth and relief, it's like meeting an old friend. I feel I am embarking on a new journey!

There is the same conflict and differences here as there was in *Sons and Lovers*—between men and women, that is. Women are allways the same ones striving for something more—looking ahead. I wonder if Lawrence thinks women are like this in all situations?

When I read the bit about "the pulse and body of the soil" first on my own, I thought it sounded really poetic and beautiful (p42), and when the more sordid meaning of it was discussed I felt quite . . . as if I'd been slapped in the face! I think I'd like to stick to my, if niave, version.

I notice "blood" is mentioned again and again. Didn't he believe in "blood feelings"? It must have been the influence of Freda—him writing about his beliefs like this. Very dangerous too, I should think!?

Mrs Morel appears again—wanting more for her children than their father had. Not only did his mother influence his earlier life—she even had an unspoken say in his writing later on. How frustrating to Freda! (I wonder if education *is* the answer?)

Hate and love, again! "they would have been heavy and uninspired and inclined to hate" p45. I will never understand how he can use the word so much and so freely.

A new type of woman—he doesn't write about these very often, "pretty dark woman, quaint in her speech, whimsical," Lawrence had probably met many more people by the time he wrote this.

Enter DH Lawrence himself . . . Tom Brangwen! I wonder how many of Tom's earlier sexual experiences were D H Lawrence's? "He knew that, in those last waves of nakedness, he did not exist to her nor she to him" p55. There he goes again! So cynnical!

Ah—the polish lady. Like Freda—foriegn, like Freda—already has a child, like Freda—older than him (Tom). Lawrence definitly has a fascination for foriegn women! I wonder if the child will cause problems between Tom and the Polish lady. What a beautiful "courtship" between them! "They were such strangers" p84. Why, oh why must he insist that men and women merely use each other and don't come to know one another? Does love/passion really hurt so much? "Such intamacy of embrace, and such utter foreigness of contact! It was unbearable" p84. I wouldn't know!

Oh, Lawrence can really write!; " . . . a high moon, liquid-brilliant, scudded across a hollow space and took cover under electric, brown—iridescent cloud-edges. Who else would describe the moon as liquid-brilliant!? I can't wait to read on. Please don't let Tom become a drunken bastard and the polish lady a bitter old woman.

Maybe it's just the mood I was in that time—but he does seem to have spent an awful lot of time at the beginning of the chapter going on about Lydia's unhappiness. I'm—well, I was—getting quite irritated with her. I like the way Lawrence continues to describe her like a flower—though at the time I think this woman would be more like a strong, thorny red rose than any other flower!

THERE HE GOES AGAIN! How annoying! "wordless passion, almost in hatred of her." Hate and passion linked again. (Just typical of a man to ask a woman to marry him, and *then* to worry about them being strangers!)

I wonder what is so ugly about her mouth.

It is sad—this foreignness between man and wife. Is marriage really like this? On p96 Tom is described as being scared that Lydia will leave him. I bet Lawrence always felt insecure about his relationship with Frieda. I suppose it prevents boredom setting in. ?!? I think the line "What did it matter who they were, whether they knew each other or not?"

(p99) is very profound—possibly the most sensible thing he has said so far!

On page 99 Lydia is described as "ugly-mouthed" again. Why describe someone as ugly-mouthed? I've seen a photograph of Frieda in a book, when Lawrence first met her—she had a curious, strong, determined face—yet a strange, slanting almost mocking smile. Would he have described it as ugly?

These two are searching for each other in their lonely marriage—and I'm desperately hoping it will all end "happily ever after." Then they will realize they love each other (a word I hasten to add, that has not been mentioned as yet.) I get the feeling, however, considering Lawrence's loathe of happy endings that this is as good as it'll get.

By the end of the chapter the woman has dominated the man yet again. "For he was afraid of his wife . . . his heart seemed under the millstone of it, . . . she . . . like the upper millstone lying on him, crushing him" p101. Is this how Lawrence really believes a relationship develops?

I love the tender, fragile relationship that Lawrence has created between Lydia's child and Brangwen. It is strange that he can portray a father/daughter relationship so vividly even though he and Frieda had no children. Lydia is having his child. I bet it's a boy.

Jo's thoughts about Chapter 8

Are the inner feelings of Will known as dark and black, it makes him look an evil man which he isn't. "From the first, the baby stirred in the young father a deep, strong emotion he dared scarcely acknowledge, it was so strong and came out of the dark of him!" Will also seems alien towards the child yet he realizes with a sick feeling that the bundle is his own flesh and blood.

The father, Will, loves the child more than any of his offspring his love has grown from strength to strength just like the baby has grown. Now that Anna has had ANOTHER baby already Will can take Ursula as his own maybe he won't feel left out because before Anna tended to Ursula and so the baby only needed its mother. Now Will can take the role of father.

Gudrun I think this is a horrid name to call a girl, it makes me think of a large fat German girl!

Anna is becoming very narrow-minded as a mother and just seeing her children and not Will. "This was enough for Anna—she seemed to pass off into a kind of rapture of motherhood, her rapture of motherhood was everything."

The relationship between Ursula and her father is very sweet, well thats what I think. Everything is perfect between them at the moment but if she has any of her mother in her she will want to be a separate individual soon. D. H. Lawrence keeps referring to something black and dark in Will and describing him as a young black cat, which gives me the impression that he creeps and is mysterious. I realize that the inner thoughts and mysteries of our minds he referes to as darkness or black because we can't see what's going on.

I like the description of Ursula from Will's view in the carpentry shed "with her presence flickering upon him." This makes me think of a little toddler running around looking at things and scooping items off the floor which are useless, just like I used to do.

A moment ago I wrote that if Ursula takes after her mother in any way she'll want to be independant, look at this "She passionately resented her mother's superficial authority. She wanted to assert her own detachment."

D. H. Lawrence uses quite a few similies to describe Will's actions and Ursula in the church "like a kitten playing by herself" and "like a bee among flowers," then her father's reaction after being told off due to her "His voice was harsh and cat-like," does that mean he was spiteful or did he meow?

This is the third child and "Anna continued in her violent trance of motherhood, always busy, often harassed, but always contained in her trance of motherhood."

Fancy having four children at the age of twenty six poor Will.

Still no boy born theres now Ursula, Gudrun, Theresa and Catherine.

Does Will never explain properly to his family why he's shouting at them, poor young Ursula never understands why he suddenly shouts at her. For example her walking across the newly sown seeds she didn't know you're not meant to do that and she gets blamed for nothing to her.

What a weird man fancy wanting to frighten your child. Throwing himself and his child off a bridge, I thought Will was much more sensible than Anna.

With Anna still being contained in her motherhood she is ignoring her husband and look now he's seeking for someone else. "He began to go away from home. He went to Nottingham on Saturdays, always alone, to the football match and to the music-hall, and all the time he was watching, in readiness."

Its taken quite a long time for Will to get to his crisis stage as the novelty of his marriage is wearing off. Tom Brangwen was getting fed up with his marriage after two years when he went alone to see his brother Alfred's mistress.

How could Will's life be barren he has children a home and his passion for the church. Now he's found a young lady in the theatre will she become his mistress or is he just curious like his father-in-law?

I think he's just curious

Is this the dark side of Will?

I'll answer my own question this is that Will definately has a dark side and that is what I have just read.

Anna reacts like her mother did when Tom returned home after seeing that woman, she sees a different man and becomes very interested in him. So this provides a new life to the married couple and the household.

Reading for Meaning

It interests me that these think-write responses, whether to novel or play—from thirteen-, fourteen- and seventeen-year-olds alike, are chiefly responses to the world that the words evoke *and not to the text as a literary artifact.* Sophie knows "how the children felt," Karen responds directly to the preacher as though he were standing there in front of her, Ashleigh wonders "Did Romeo really love Ros?" and Jemma pleads "Please don't let Tom become a drunken bastard and the polish lady a bitter old woman."

In this respect they come into the first of Purves and Rippere's "relationships" with a literary work: "engagement-involvement," the direct interacting of reader and work which they acknowledge is often the object of pedagogical disdain (*Elements of Writing about a Literary Work*). One might have hoped after the lively debates between structuralists "post" and "neo," which have stimulated university English departments for the last couple of decades that such a toffee-nosed attitude to student readers of literature would have ameliorated somewhat. Depressingly, I see little sign of change in the criteria for acceptable literary response that the Examining Boards are currently promulgating, with their stress on "critical appreciation" and "judgment."

These logs do of course reveal a wider range of responses to the texts in question than a purely engagement-involvement relationship. They show an awareness that what is under consideration is the work of another writer and that he or she has been responsible for decisions about plot and character. From time to time they also show the capacity to relate patterns of significance in their personal world with patterns in the writer's "heterocosm," as when Jemma writes "Why, oh why must he insist that men and women merely use each other and don't come to know one another? Does love/passion really hurt so much? Such intimacy of embrace, and such utter foreignness of contact! It was unbearable (p.84). I wouldn't know!"

It is true that none of these entries is judgmental and one could say that journal writing makes no demands on the writer to evaluate. I would want to argue that the expectation that these young writers and readers should sit in judgment is equally out of place in their formal essay writing—as it would be for most of us who do not have the temerity to pursue literary criticism as a profession. More meaningful surely to engage with and to interpret the text both as a lone reader and in the shared but undogmatic discussion of our perceptions with those of others.

Recursive Responses to "The Arrival of the Bee Box"

This awareness of a range of possible responses that can be made to a text is even more evident in the "recursive" journal writing of this same group of students when they were invited to make three entries on three separate but closely linked occasions, for encounters with the same poem.

The Arrival of the Bee Box

I ordered this, this clean wood box
Square as a chair and almost too heavy to lift.
I would say it was the coffin of a midget
Or a square baby
Were there not such a din in it.

The box is locked, it is dangerous.
I have to live with it overnight
And I can't keep away from it.
There are no windows, so I can't see what is in there.
There is only a little grid, no exit.

I put my eye to the grid.
It is dark, dark,
With the swarmy feeling of African hands
Minute and shrunk for export,
Black on black, angrily clambering.

How can I let them out?
It is the noise that appalls me most of all,
The unintelligible syllables.
It is like a Roman mob,
Small, taken one by one, but my god, together!

I lay my ear to furious Latin.
I am not a Caesar.
I have simply ordered a box of maniacs.
They can be sent back.
They can die, I need feed them nothing, I am the owner.

I wonder how hungry they are.
I wonder if they would forget me
If I just undid the locks and stood back and turned into a tree.
There is the laburnum, its blond colonnades,
And the petticoats of the cherry.

They might ignore me immediately
In my moon suit and funeral veil.
I am no source of honey
So why should they turn on me?
Tomorrow I will be sweet God, I will set them free.

The box is only temporary.

The group were asked initially to free write their immediate response to the poem (they were not given the name of the poet, Sylvia Plath), in any way they liked for about ten minutes. They were then asked to spend up to thirty minutes making a second response (to find out what further thoughts occurred to them) for homework—and after discussion in class following this second entry, to make a third response, noting any changes in their ideas, but with the recognition that there was no "right answer"—and therefore no particular pressure for group consensus.

For lack of space, I will only quote the consecutive journal entries that were made by two of the students, although each set of encounters was refreshingly individual—and thoughtful. I got the strong impression that every reader approached the poem as they might a mysterious object, turning it round and round in their minds as they scrutinized it for its hidden significance—and searching their own lives for any experience that might help to shed light on the inner meanings of the poem.

Julie wrote:

(1) I like the words "square as a chair" Prison cell. "Minute and shrunk for export"—slave trade? "Furious Latin" "unintelligible sylla-bles"—maybe the person is scared of foreign people. Prejudice is supposed to derive from fear . . .

(2) Is a beebox used for transporting bees? If it is it would have a small grid. "In my moon suit and funeral veil." Bee keepers wear veil type hats. Moon suits remind me of the people who wear antiradioactivity suits.

If I'm right about the box containing slaves or black people under apartheid then I suppose the connection with bees makes sense. You keep bees in a beebox and they are in your power but although small and not so intelligent (do not think I am racist. I am writing from the subject's view.) they can still sting. Slaves or the South Africans are kept in a type of box. Slaves are also owned.

"Small, taken one by one, but my God, together!" bee stings don't hurt that much but if five thousand chased you it would kill you. I suppose these people like President Botha consider this. If a couple of black people cause trouble he'll have his policemen beat them up but if every single black person went against him he wouldn't have a chance.

After the person's worrying they reassure themselves with "they can die, I need feed them nothing, I am the owner." Even if it was just bees and not people that someone was referring to its still nasty. The laburnum is a flowering tree with yellow groups of flowers. According to my Dad not many people know that the seeds are poisonous. Is this why the person would turn into a laburnum. I suppose it would suit them. "I am no source of honey"—back to the bee thing again. Maybe meaning "they can't get anything from me" or "Why would the black people want to get me?"

"The box is only temporary" will they break out or will he let go?

I'm not sure though, if I forget all about the black people and just think about bees it must be pretty scarey for the person. He wants to let them go but they'll attack him if he does. This could show us how some people in South Africa feel. Afterall some of them must think twice and figure maybe it wasn't such a good idea afterall. Anyway, all the bees want is out of that bloomin beebox and so do the black people want an end to apartheid.

It sounds stupid but this person sums up how I sometimes feel. I keep fish and I worry about them in their tank. Should I let them go or will they die or be eaten. I hate it when one dies because I always think they may have committed suicide because they're so bored in that tank (I know it sounds stupid). I feel a bit of sympathy for the bloke with the beebox but I think the bees have a worse deal than him or my fish.

(3) The box seems like a great burden on the person. I suppose I can understand the person's point of view and feel some sympathy for him because we only hear his thoughts, not the bees inside. I'm not sure

about my apartheid theory, it all fits but it seems like I only thought of it because of "swarmy feeling of African hands." Another clue is "box of maniacs." Surely noone could call bees maniacs. Maniacs is much too human a word.

"Minute and shrunk for export" isn'i a very nice phrase. It makes me think of slaves again. Like they've been freeze dried and packed or something. The image of a shrunk African hand that is all swarmy and clamy is like one of those wierd charm things that Witchdoctors wore. Tribesmen in parts of Africa wear odd charms. I saw some on television with all sorts of bits, dried and put round their necks.

It's quite a frightening poem. If I ignore any of my theories about metaphors and things and just think about bees I can really understand this person. If I had a beebox I'd be too scared to let the bees out. I've seen too many cartoons where they form an arrow and chase people into lakes and ponds.

Like a "Roman mob." Romans used to have thousands of men in each group and thousands of groups in each legion and thousands of legions in each army and millions of armies to fight each battle. No wonder the person is scared. The white people who belive in apartheid in South Africa are only a minority but they have guns. This is like the beekeeper with his five million bees in a box, they could kill him but he has the food.

I think I do like my South African theory. It all seems to fit so well.

I suppose though this poem could fit with all sorts of things. Any prisoners. Maybe it's like Amnesty International. Political prisoners and writers locked up and that sort of thing. Then again writers aren't usually like a Roman mob or a box of maniacs and anyway there aren't millions of them.

I shall stick to the apartheid one.

Marianne wrote:

(1) It's strange that bees are sent through the post! But then again I do remember the Rural Studies teacher saying that you can order bees if you are an avid beekeeper. I wonder why someone would write a poem about a bee box? The poem does convey the author's fascination—trying to look inside, listening to the noise. I don't understand the line "With the swarmy feeling of African hands." I like the sentence "I have simply ordered a box of maniacs." The poor bees, being boxed up like that!

I'm running out of time, my thoughts are rushed and I'm not conveying them very well. First of all wonders if they will ignore him—as if he didn't want them to, then he says "Why should they turn on me?" Is he more worried about them escaping or stinging him? Why won't he set them free *now?* They might die!

I missed the "moon suit and funeral veil." If I had enough time, I could make more sense of it.

(2) I like the sound of "bee box," the actual words said together. The poem seems really controlled—very orderly—not over emotional, not rushing to say too much. In fact, I'd never have imagined an article, any article could inspire such thoughts. I suppose it must be a real gift to be

able to convey and express feelings and thoughts without making them seem stupid. "Square as a chair," that's a strange thing to compare a wooden box to...I'd never have thought a chair was especially square! The beebox is obviously fascinating. It reminds me about an A A Milne poem about a beetle in a matchbox! Having a living thing in possession. I don't understand "With the swarmy feeling of African hands, minute and shrunk for export." Why would African hands be exported? Is this a reference to the slave trade—when African natives were locked up in ships in such dark conditions too?

It is amazing that she actually compares the box of bees to a "Roman Mob"!! Perhaps that is how she imagined a Roman Mob to be, when she was reading Shakespeare!

"A box of maniacs"—I like that. She brings to mind exactly how the bees sound, "Angry, furious, maniacs." I don't really understand the line "I wonder if they would forget me if I just undid the locks and stood back and turned into a tree." Why would they remember a tree, anyway? It seems a really strange thing to think, or say (or write!) Then she turns to trees—its as if this is just her mind wandering.

I still don't understand the "moon suit and funeral veil" bit. If she was a tree, why would she be in a moon suit and funeral veil? I suppose moon refers to night, and funeral refers to...death? They both seem to link with the word "black." So is it night time? I don't think I'm any the wiser! I like the phrase though. "Moon suit and funeral veil." Only to me, the moon makes me think of a glowing light and stars...not particularly of dark. Why does she wait until tomorrow before setting them free? She's curious yet she won't let them out. Why did she order them in the first place, if she was only going to set them free? Perhaps she is a bee keeper. I don't think so.

"Setting them free" as opposed to locking them up. Makes me think of the African slaves again.

It's strange that a God who sets people free is "sweet." Like honey! What I mean is that it's a strange word to use. I would expect it to be, good, kind, loving, merciful...not sweet!

I don't think she is ever going to set them free, even if the poem ends with "the box is only temporary."

(3) Some sense of my thoughts on the poem? It is a poem about a bee box. The poet is obviously fascinated with it, she looks at it, listens to it, tries to see inside it, in fact "can't keep away from it."

I think also that the poem has a theme of captivation (obviously) shown not only in the fact that the bees are boxed, but also by referring to the slave trade. For example "with the swarmy feeling of African hands minute and shrunk for export." I think maybe now that I have looked at it for the third time, that the "hand" is not a word for part of the body, but used instead of "help." Like a servent, a worker. Or a slave. I am still not sure as to wether this is a poem that just refers to slavery... or wether slavery is the main theme.

I do know though, that the poem is very much concerned with captivation, locking someone or something up; having control and being the owner. The owner of the bees could starve them too. Or he could set them free. I suppose in this exercise I am not trying to discover the impossible—what the poet meant; but what it means to me. And if I say what it means to me—can it be wrong? NO!

Therefore I'll be positive. To me, this is a poem that on the surface seems just another nice uncomplicated poem that's fairly straightforward—with a few confusing lines thrown in; they might be confusing but they sound good. Yet, when the poem is dug into, pondered on, rediscovered—then it has a much more serious theme. To those who can see it, it is about the slavery of others, the power some people have to lock someone or something up.

To me, I think the poet has no intention of setting the bees free at all ... Maybe that means that slavery—the monopoly some people have over others—will not end. But then, maybe the last line does have a glimmer of hope in it for the future. "The box is only temporary." Yes, I think it does have hope in it. I have changed my mind; the box *is* only temporary.

I think, to be able to slip a serious theme into an apparently straightforward, seemingly simple poem is extremely clever. (But too much work for the reader!!)

I don't think that Marianne is taking the micky here when she declares stoutly that she is setting out to find her own meanings for the poem and therefore cannot be criticized for "getting it wrong." I am sure that their teacher has talked to the group about "no right answers" and it is this reminder to her teacher that genuinely does give Marianne the heart to be positive—to summarize her understanding so far—and to feel free to change her mind at the last minute.

I enjoy the way both girls are willing in their writing to unpack, repack, and unpack again the possible meanings that this "bee box" contains. I also like the way that they are still thinking about the poem third time around—still discovering further interpretations. If I had been able to join them for a discussion after reading their entries this far, I would have suggested perhaps that metaphor enables a poet to suggest many meanings as they reverberate from a specific moment in time, such as Sylvia Plath standing in front of the box of bees that she has ordered and must now make decisions about. But the girls are getting there anyway—Julie when she suddenly realizes, "I suppose though, this poem could fit with all sorts of things" and Marianne in her final comment—joking apart!

As an alternative to essay writing, I have no doubt that journal writing has given these writers a freedom and a confidence to explore their own thoughts—and in doing so, the texts to which they have been addressing themselves, which taking on the role of literary critic could only impede. These writers are not concerned primarily with *form;* they are concerned primarily with *meaning.* Examiners may quarrel with that priority but I doubt whether any of the authors would.

The Stories Behind the Stories

The entries which follow come from the journals of two seventeen-year-old students at the start of their Advanced Level English Literature

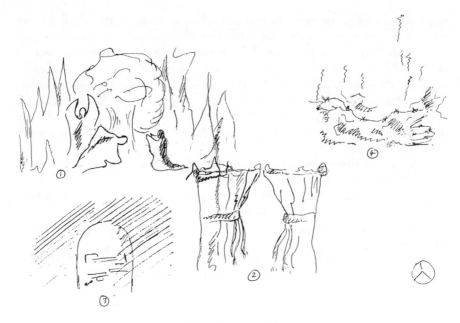

Figure 7–1   Emma's Sketches

course, taught jointly at their school by two teachers who were piloting a new modular scheme. I am interested in the detailed picture of their efforts to compose a short story, which evolves from their own reflections over half a term; I hope that these excerpts will capture this intermeshing of "writing to make sense" with "writing to make," as unfortunately there isn't the space here to quote either their entire logs or their entire stories. Both girls certainly convinced me that the think-writing helped to sustain their draftings and redraftings as they composed. It is interesting also to note how all five helical capacities have been brought into play: thinking, feeling, verbalizing, visualizing and doing or enacting.

Emma-Mapping Work in Progress

14.9.87

Before the lesson today I had seen a newspaper articale on nuclear war and nuclear disarmement. Despite wanting to base my ideas today on the ideas which developed from the previous lesson ie. surprise endings and murder I found all my visions being based on nuclear war. (Something which I know very little about)

Originally I went to the hall to develop ideas with a musical instrument but instead I looked at the stage and ideas developed which I sketched first [see Figure 7–1] and then made these notes about:

Written as reality   1. *Several people dancing in flames, a scene of distruction include mushroom clouds. The figures have no features emphasizing they are no one imperticular*

Surprised

2. *The curtains closing.*
3. *The opening of the basement door where the rehearsal for the production has been.*
4. *Only to see the world in distruction ie. leaving you to think either the world has been destroyed or maybe an accident has taken place there—nobody is to know.*

For the next month, Emma experimented in her journal with ideas for her story, drafting and redrafting different parts of it as new ideas came to her—sometimes from other short stories that she was reading and discussing in the course of this A-level module. For instance on 10/14/87 her entry reads:

> **More re-reading of Nuclear Idea.** The boy is acting "too big for his boots" not many boys of 12 would confront a man with a gun. Maybe he should be older or it should be a girl—maybe a pregnant Mum, or Mum with child so more should be written into the final lines (speach) of the play part of the story.
>
> **Ending**—the door opened to the wide world outside the rehearsing basement. There was an unusual odor outside, the air was dull and used, hands of dancing faceless figures clasped burning throats—(just like the beginning of the story.)

Later the same day in a further English lesson with the other teacher working on the module, Emma wrote in her journal:

> (*At the Railway Station, Upway* by Thomas Hardy) I have no reason for writing out this poem apart from I realy liked it. The whole atmosphere catches and involves me in the situation—this type of atmosphere could maybe be used in the lonely man idea—.
>
> The little boy—the pitied child who has nothing but his violin and the happiness which it brings him—maybe an idea for the boy in the nuclear play. I liked the idea of innocence and misfortune "There is not much that I can do, For I've no money thats quite my own!"—this is great, full of emotion and feeling in simple words.

On 10/19/87 Emma wrote:

> Decided after thought about the speach at end of the nuclear story that it should be made by a girl or mother so that more can be read into the "play" about life etc. Also payed some attention to a title for the story. Ideas, "The Close of the Curtain," "The End," "The final ending"

Here is the beginning of her first version of a girl being the final human character in the play that is being acted out on the basement stage:

> A girl of about 18 climbed from the rubble of a building above which stood a bent sign with letters SPT Centre on it. It was the sports centre. [There is a cross against this and Emma starts again]

A girl of about 18 climbed from the rubble of a building burnt and scarred. Her hair was burnt and tumbled over in front of her deep lifeless eyes. Her dress was torn and her knees scabby and splashed in blood. In her burnt arms lay a bundle of melting cloth, a scarred shapeless lump lay within.

Eight weeks into the module, Emma's log has become a mixture of reflections and trial drafts for parts of the story. At this point, which is where we must leave her, she has written two alternative versions for the ending, the first moving into the outside world beyond the play, the second terminating with a tableau effect before the final curtain.

First ending

A young girl with metal rimmed glasses took out a tape measure and began taking down numbers as she measured up and down various garments. Actors clambered from the scenery and figures in colorless costumes disappeared into changing rooms. Dancers took off ballet shoes and changed into casual clothes. A group began to form near the front of the stage where electronic musical equipment was being stacked.

"Is everyone ready" asked a girl in blue legwarmers and a pair of jeans with holes in the knees.

The group of about twenty moved casually to the cellar door. The lights were switched off and the cellar door opened. Instead of the bright street-lights and cool winter night they expected, the air was dull and used, hands of dancing faceless figures grasped burning throats . . .

Second ending

The girl stood up, her singing stopped and there was silence.

"I," she gulped in the (muggy) air "I am Carline, Carline Shaw I was in the center of the basement when . . .

"You should be dead" he took the gun and pointed it at her. He used the tip of the gun to pull the clothes away from the bundle she held. She snatched it away. "That's right, just you try, not only are you satisfied with destroying the world, killing my baby, you now want its dead corpse, You. You. You! What gives you the right to destroy my world, the world God created, the world I loved. What are you to take the lives of innocent children, to murder my baby, my love, my baby. How can you sleep knowing that half the world lays dead and numb with its creations destroyed, here she flung the bundle at him. "Take all I have, take it, I hate you"

A ringing shot sounded in the settling mist. The girl winced in pain, knelt choking on her own blood. Another shot winced into her body and she fell on the uphurled earth. The man stood his gun pointing out to the world . . . .

The Curtain Closed

The last log entry that I have for Emma reads:

28.10.87—I don't know wheather to include the end about the curtain etc or just simply to concentrate on the nuclear war and the girl's feelings to the man—the gun being pointed at the world...brings new ideas and feelings about him and those who use nuclear weapons to destroy.

Katie's Commentary on Her Emerging Story

Katie was working in the same group as Emma, and her "funeral" story arises out of some dramatic improvisations about a man who exposed himself, which the group worked on together in the first week of term and then wrote about briefly from the point of view of one of the characters involved:

This lesson I felt was really quite useful to show how emotions and actions can play a very large part in our lifes without us even realising. In our pairs we had to firstly tell each other about an experience we had had in our life which was embarassing or one which we should like to forget. It quickly became apparent that it did not really matter what the story was but how it had affected the person and what emotions he or she had encountered. The group who eventually watched the mimes were able to readily pick up the main theme of the tale just by the actions. It was interesting to see how each individual interpreted the actions.

I wrote: "The sickening sight seemed to firstly amuse the girls but this was quickly overtaken by surprise. Within the next few minutes, embrassement set in before the lasting effect of disgust took control. With no thought for consequences the offender seemed to gain a sense of pride in what he was doing."

Possible ideas for short story writing came into my head—Perhaps—brother and sister seeking revenge on their father who abused them as children? (or other people). Father can be built up as a sorrowful, pityful, sad character—possibly divorcee or widower. Maybe more interesting if you had to deal with his wife's emotions? Perhaps children have lost touch—used to be very close. Remember those times when they first meet.

Ending—father dies before any revenge is gained. But ending paragraph hints towards the son doing exactly what his father did.

Daughter finds relationships difficult. She felt cold and unyielding towards him.

Could start with funeral and then flashback—perhaps too ordinary?

Tuesday, 15th September

I can see a real possibility from the conversation after the funeral. I think I will forget the revenge theme and the idea of the rose garden, I think I may keep for development later on.

Tuesday, 29th September

My writing really progressed today and I was very pleased with the story development of the funeral. I am writing a piece about the scene after a funeral concentrating on the thoughts of a few people in the room. The opening description I thought was very powerful but I hope the story doesn't just turn into a descriptive piece. I have found it useful to ask different people what ideas they have of funerals. Words such as, falseness, tension, atmosphere, loss, sadness have all come up. Throughout the story I want to keep the idea of an intimidating silence in the room and how each of the characters react to this silence. I'm not quite sure how the story will end but at the moment I am just writing out paragraphs, describing each character and their thoughts.

Date?

I'm not sure that my funeral story is going exactly the way I wanted it to—I'm not emphasizing the silence enough and I feel that the taboo subject of the man's past is not coming through. The scene between the 2 old women is a start to how the other relatives reacted to the man and what he did—but I also feel that perhaps the conversation is too boring. Unfortunately I seem to have lost the powerful writing that I started with! I hope the scenes link up with each other.

In the event Katie produced a carefully crafted and very successful short story. After several interlocking conversations have taken place over the cold meats, the final figure to appear is that of the son:

A figure stood menacingly in the doorway blocking any entrance to or from the room. Slowly the haunting outline moved among the crowds, making each one of them turn to look. The silhouette viewed the room remembering the sickening sight which had confronted him all those years ago; he remembered the embrassment which had been his first reaction before the lasting effect of disgust and realisation had taken control. He dwelled on the arguments, their consequences and then he could only think about his mother's horror as he unfolded the story to her—the disbelief, the agony and then—he felt the memories stab him like the crudest murder weapon.
The silence began to rest on him as he made his way towards one individual standing by the window. As he stood in front of this woman, he looked comfortingly at her and then in a soft voice said "Mum?"
With this Jan looked up, to see the mature face of her son and deep, deep inside her she was filled with an agonising sense of knowing.

It seems to me that reflective think-writing of the kind that Katie and Emma have produced throughout this sequence of lessons, reveals their commitment to the business of story writing, which can in itself, be valued and taken seriously as an illuminating learning process. Not only are they mapping their own progress thoughtfully and seriously, because that map is made in writing—through a sequence of journal entries, they can share it with their teacher, revealing in a highly "context specific" way, the story behind the growth of their stories. I would want this writing to receive weighting in their final assessment at the end of the course, along with the finished pieces to which it relates. It reveals very clearly their awareness of form—and how form affects meaning. Even if their finished stories are still not a hundred percent successful (and how many professional writers would want to make that claim for themselves?) these students have revealed in the process of describing their efforts as story-makers a concern, a commitment and an understanding which should receive both recognition and commendation.

Looking Back at Work Undertaken in Class

In one sense I suppose any journal writing which is either recollective or reflective can be said to offer a writer the opportunity to look back, either over what is already known before new work can commence or over work in progress to sort out confusions, ask questions, make predictions and so forth.

What I want to offer more specifically here, are examples of log entries which have been written to let the teacher know the pupil's thoughts and feelings about activities recently undertaken in class. Mostly these entries are fairly brief but they can provide the teacher with very useful information about individual hopes and fears, satisfactions and frustrations which might never otherwise be shared. Where they have been included, I quote the teacher's responses.

Kenny—a thirteen-year-old who is still withdrawn from some lessons for special-needs help

I thought that I DiD very well in the spider plans as you say. I thought that the pictures which you had TO DO and SAY what they DiD for a Liveing were a Bit harD TO DO.

I Like Doing Topics they are very GooD. I Like the one we did on ISreal. I Like Reading my mate ShofIQ I also Like doing the thing about the paties[?] I like the Film.

I'm glad you like doing topics. Is that because you can get on at your own pace and choose what you want to do?

I LiKE What we HAVE Been Doing with MAPS AND MAKING the Models of old Town. I LiKe the talk about HONG KONG. I would LiKe to start a New Book to Read for the whole class.

We will be starting a new book in September. There isn't time to do a whole one now but I will see if I can find a few short stories. Your model worked out well didn't it?

YeS. I LiKe the BooK we are reading it is good. I LiKe doing some of the watch house work But some is a Bit hard to Do. I LiKe making the map out of tiles. I also like doing the detatives sheets they where fun.

You are doing well at the moment Kenny. Don't worry if you find some things a bit hard! Stretching your brain is good for it!

Sonia—a lively thirteen-year-old in the same class as Kenny

I have enjoyed doing this section of work it is quite fun. I loved the idea of having faces as good, bad and O.K.

Another thing I liked about it is that you had to use the evidence again when you done the first part. I liked doing the second part as well putting the four most important people in your life into one, two, three and four. It really got you going about who you were going to put first.

We have done some more graph work which I am pleased at because I enjoy graph work. I have enjoyed doing the poems as well.

I have also enjoyed doing the faces booklet, that has been quite fun really.

The commentry on my lifetime I quite enjoyed doing that but it wasn't as good as the rest of what we have been doing. I think I have done quite well in this section of work because if I enjoy doing a section of work then I really try and do the best that I can do.

I'm very glad you have enjoyed it so much Sonia. I have certainly enjoyed reading your work. Your presentation is immaculate and you make very helpful comments.

There isn't really a lot to report on, I have once again enjoyed everything, I think henge [Humanities and English] is my favorite subject If only I could get the things right.

I am not very good at writing stories so of course the one I'm writing at the moment is rubbish, but I think it's a Brilliant idea about doing it on the computer. I think the things that we are doing on the relief of Old Town are quite good, but I wish we could hurry up and get onto something better. Why do we have to do what I think the school say we have to do. Can't the class chose what they want to do, do their own topic like we did when we done the research.

I'd do some research on old churches, I really enjoy doing research work, I think I could do that all year round.

Are you worried about getting things wrong? I'm never really aware of you getting much wrong and often there isn't just one right answer! Why don't you like the relief work on Old Town? Don't you like map work? You don't have to do what the school says all the time—there's really quite a lot of choice built in!

Readers may have noted that this teacher's replies are fairly liberally sprinkled with question marks and exclamation marks, rather as a letter to a friend might be. It is my impression that this is characteristic of teacher responses to pupils' journals. The punctuation is signaling the teacher's own interest and concern in a way that facial or hand gestures would do in speech. Reading it "cold" like this in print carries a hint of Joyce Grenfell gush. But this is misleading; where the writer is known to the pupil the translation to how her comments would sound in talk can easily be made.

I also like the way she responds *positively* to each pupil, taking on a partnership role which notes their suggestions about lessons as well as supporting their efforts to date.

Weighing It All Up

This class of twelve-year-olds had been finding out about a variety of ethnic groups, working in twos or threes. Here are some of the comments that they logged for their teacher at the end of the topic:

Eskimos

I thought it was good doing the Prodject I would like to do another Prodject. about something diferent. I liked seaching for it then writing it all down. it was very interesting. Yes I think we did a bit actually. We could of learned a bit more if we read through a hole book of eskimos. I enjoyed working with the other two but I would like to do a Prodject on my own. if we all work on our own and we all do something different and we can do it at home it would be more interesting and better than groups.

Aborigines Project

I enjoyed researching and writing up the project. I especially liked the drawing because they were interesting and really different than in England. I think that we definately learnt alot. I hardly knew anything about Aborigines when we started this and now I know things like what they eat and language.

I think working in groups more than two can be a bit hectic so I worked with my best friend. By working in larger groups, you can be tempted to talk and not do much work. Working alone can be okay too, but it might be better to exchange information. I think that we could have done with more resources like a video or more books. What we had was alright but we could have used it well and done a lot more for it.

I think that exchanging information is alright because people who have different information might not have the stuff that you have.

North American Indians (1)

I enjoyed doing my project on the North American Indians. As I had been to America and through Indian country I wanted to find out more. I prefered writing the information than researching it because I prefer writing. I was surprised at how much there was to learn about the

Indians, much more than I thought. I would have liked to watch a television program which might have told me more. I think it is better to work with someone else sometimes because you can confer about ideas. I would have liked to have used more books than I did so I could put the books together and use all the information.

When I had to share my research with other people I felt I had the confidence to talk about the Indians fluently. I was able to answer all the questions that people asked and even go into more detail sometimes. I found it quite easy listening to other people talk about their projects and they gave me the answers to the questions I asked. I think I learnt alot from other people's information, more than I knew before. I think it was a good idea to exchange research because it widened other people's knowledge.

North American Indians (2)

I enjoyed the project alot and it was quite interesting. The information finding was the fun part but when it came to writing up it took a long time. Even though the writing was boring I did find out alot about North American Indians. Myself I think that projects are the best way to learn things because you batter it into you with writing it. I was surprised at the amount of books there was on them and there was easly enough for the project. Working with someone is a good thing because you can find things out and put them together to find out more.

Working It Out

John often appeared to be quite a feckless kid—the type that forgot to bring what he needed to lessons and then wandered round the class distracting other kids. His handwriting was in fact handprinting; it looked slapdash and quite often letters were missed out in his rush to get the boring business of writing over and done with. I was asked to do what I could to help John improve his writing when he was at the start of his third year. I decided to introduce him to the idea of "writing to think" in a journal of his own, in the hope that this would give writing more status in his eyes and thus encourage him to take it more seriously as a worthwhile activity.

For several months we posted this think-book back and forth to each other. Sometimes J's printing was produced in a firm clear hand; at other times it became distorted speed printing—though never illegible. I am not sure whether keeping up this correspondence at a distance had any permanent effect on J's attitude to writing but over that period he produced an interesting range of thoughtful entries about his own "progress" of which these are a selection.

First entry—J sets out to explain why he is "slow" at reading and writing:

At C school the only English we had was taking words home and reading, but I sometimes never use to bother learning them and sometimes

I never read. In the first year at S School, we started useing books. I russ through the books because I did not like English, and we still read books but I sometimes never read.

All through the 2nd year we had a chose of either math or English and I done maths most off the time. Only some times I don English.

In the 3rd year we had to do English just as mush as maths but I just mess around when I done English and I hardly read.

In the 4th year I rushed my work because if we done our work before the end off the day we could draw and paint, so I rust my work. We had reading time but I read slowly. As for my spelling I never use to leren the word I just keept on asking my mates.

In the first year (at secondary school) I went to the remidal every lesson. In the remidal I worked very hard I didn't west time I consentred hard to improve my Reading. My age off reading when I went into the remidal was about 7 to 8 years old at the end of the frist year I was 10 years old at reading when I should of bin 11, so I went in the remidal in the 2nd year but it has only one lesson a week. I improved alot so that I took a test to get out of there and I passed. So I am coming out of the remidal in the 3rd year.

In my lessons with the rest of my class I talked a lot and distracted others. But I done my directions work quiet fast. And I mest around alot, but I think I've got better now.

My response:

Thank you for writing in so much detail. I'm interested in everything you have to say John—especially about why you dislike reading and writing! I think you only start to enjoy doing anything when it becomes important to you in some way or another.

Reading I enjoy, because it helps me to cut off from all the other things I ought to be doing (!!).

Writing is very important to me because it really does help me to think— or to find out what my brain's been up to while I've been occupied with other things.

Over the course of the next two terms, J wrote about what he did (or didn't) do in lessons, the struggle that he had deciding on his "options" and accounts of various activities undertaken outside school:

I was thinking about school in the 3rd year. I was thinking about working harder and I must keep out of troble. I was thinking about in maths and combind scince were it is going to be realy hard and I must consentrat. I was thinking about not getting up so eraly in the morning for my paper round. I was thinking about how am I going to get my posters up on the wall without piling the paint of the wall.

This week in math I was really really really stuck with quadrilaterals. All through the lasson I was stuck, I ask my friends they told me but I still didn't get it, this weny on for about 2–3 lessons. But in the end I asked the teacher and I now understand it and I have got a test tomorrow.

In seramicks we had to draw a picture in a book because I forgot my apron, and I had to right about the picture I drawed a famous pot. We had to finish it for home work so I look in the Library in town and found a book of it.

I am very keen on all sorts of sports. I play for the school at football, Rugby, basketball and cricket. I like football the most because I get a lot of glory when I score and when I win cups. I've all ways supported Liverpool football club ever since I was little. I play for S United now but I used to play for my old school and for the cubs. I don't wish to take football up as a career but I wouldn't mind playing part time.

I am very sorry that this entry is a bit late but I have been thinking and worrying about my options. Every day for the last past two weeks, we have had talks every morning about different subjects . . . We have to have Math, English and Games and we have to pick a science subject as well; the others were up to us to pick. We had to tick one subject from each column and put a R for another for reserve. I have not picked mine yet but I am still thinking about it . . . I want to be a policeman so I need Math and English GCSE and two others. There is a new thing it is called *modlar courses*. Modulor courses is about doing different topics . . . We have to do Information Technology and compulsory careers and then we have to pick 4 others, I am going to pick fishing, motor cycling, shooting and sporting.

In the end J chose Physics, Construction, Technology and History for his four options. He stopped writing his think-book for me when he moved into the 4th year to start his GCSE courses. What worried me about J—and still worries me about others like him is that quite misleading assumptions seemed to have been made about his *capacities* to make sense and to shape meaning because he didn't write joined-up handwriting and what he did write was "slapdash." In addition he had come along to his secondary school with a record of a so-called "reading age" of seven to eight, which had immediately consigned him for the whole of the first year to the remedial group. I would contend that J is no more "remedial" than I am—but like all learners he needs to have his interest captured so that he is *motivated* to put his mind to the topic. And of course, there is nothing that breeds success like success! Look at J's sporting record compared to his literacy record. What this lad needed was for his teachers to pay serious attention to the thoughts and feelings which lay *behind* the words on the page—to writing as a learning process as well as to writing as a code.

Casting a Critical Eye: Self-Appraisal

Andrew was lucky. He had a PE teacher who encouraged him at regular intervals to look back over the previous few weeks and evaluate his own progress. Over a period of two years these observations formed the basis of each pupil's termly report for parents. Here are some of the comments that Andrew made about himself in his second and third terms at secondary school:

16th January

Rugby

I can play Rugby quite well because I am good at running and weaving around players. I am also good at tackling because I can stretch for the legs of my opponent.

I am not very good at a scrum because I can't keep my balance.

Cross Country

I can do cross-country very well because I have a good pace for long distance running.

I didn't like getting a stitch in the middle of my run.

Basketball

I enjoy playing basketball very well because I have good judgement for shooting and am a good space finder. I didn't (find) anything difficult but I'm not tall enough to block shots.

Gymnastics

I can do rolls jumps and headstands very well because I am quite strong. I found headstands hard to perform because I didn't have the balance.

Things Outside School

I play football every Saturday for S.R.E. (Well it depends what the weathers like.) I also go swimming every fortnight.

9th Feb. Taking Part Regularly

I get to know people well by playing football with them. And I always keep up my hopes if I am losing. I am quite fit because I play many games which contain a lot of running. If I didn't take part regularly I would not have a lot of strength and skill because many people tend to forget when they have learnt something worth knowing about the game. I like to keep fit because that is an important part of being good at football and rugby and other sports. I have increased my strength by doing gymnastics.

1st May Teamwork

Advantages

In most team sports it is better to work as a team because if you try to do it individually you can run out of breath but if you work as a team and encourage your team you could get pride for winning. In a team you have a lot of advantages of making friends. I think I am good enough to be a leader in soccer because I like to encourage my team even though we are losing. I also wouldn't shout at them and boss them around because they might stop trying their best. It doesn't really matter if someone makes a mistake as long as they try their best.

Disadvantages

I think that arguing in a game leads to nowhere, because it just lets members of your team down. I don't like to be led by a bossy leader because if you make a mistake they blame it all on you even though you tryed your best.

How do I fit in?

I enjoy doing team work because you can work together and share the glory of winning and you can make friends easier. It is much easier to win than work by yourself.

Writing to Reformulate

In the following examples we can see both primary and secondary learners using writing to recollect and to reconstruct "new" knowledge. None are being required to write as though they were experts. In every case the teacher has acknowledged that the group is in the process of reaching for new understanding which is as yet incomplete.

What Makes a Car Go?

The first three entries come from a class of seven-year-olds who had been talking about how a car works with their teacher and had been out into the playground with her to peer under the bonnet of her 2CV. When they returned to the classroom, she suggested that they all have a go at putting into writing how they thought a car works.

Elizabeth is succinct:

A car has to have a engine and a battery. And you have to give it oil and water like cats food. It has to have a bonnet like the [?]. The battery gave the power.

Charlotte is clearly drawing on what she saw her teacher *doing* when she opened up the bonnet!

All cars need oil or esle they won't start. You must always put your petorl in the funny hole. to see what the matter is you lift up the bonit and wiggle the dipsick about in the bonit.

Hannah produced one of the longest think-writes:

I don't realy know how a car works but I know a little bit about it. first of al a car will Need an engine befor you can even start a car. Well you turn the kee and this piston toches some oil and it makes a spark then it goes up and down a(nd) cogs go round and round and they make the weels go round and round. if you want the car to go back wards it Does the same but the piston goes down and up. there are three pedals and I know what they are called gear pedel. breck. igselarator. you have to press butons to make the car Do serton things like make the windscreen wipas go or the beep.

Figure 7–2 Hannah's Drawing of an Engine

Her teacher wrote:

> *I think you know a lot of things Hannah. Could you draw me an engine?*
> [Hannah's drawing appears in Figure 7–2.]

For me, these entries and the ones which follow raise a very important pedagogical point. If we believe that children can always *begin* to make sense of the new and the strange, given that their recollective and reconstructive mental capacities are brought into play—then the world is their oyster! That burden of anxiety that teachers sometimes feel, that their pupils must "get it right" (to prove that their own job has been done adequately), can be tumbled off. Think-writing in fact, provides the teacher who is interested in learning with much more useful information about her pupils' current understandings than any number of tick-the-boxes. Their think-writes help her to respond individually according to their needs.

Neighboring Numbers (2/3 = 5; 5/6/7 = 18, etc.)

The next efforts to make sense through reformulation come from a class of eight- and nine-year-olds. Their task had been to find out how many of the numbers 1 through 28 could be made up by two, three or four neighboring numbers. The whole class were lined up in the school hall, holding their individual numbers on a large square of card in front of them. As you will see from the entries that I quote, some children were able to do little more than record what happened while others are teasing out mathematical patterns from the results they obtained—although why *particular* numbers can't be done remains unfathomed.

Today Mrs D,arcy came in she picked me and noone could add up to me in neiighboring number. I was 16. After lunch still no one had found out my number some people said that I was a mistrairey number I liked the neighboring numbers and I like numbers a lot. I can,t make 2,4,8,16. (Andrew)

This morning our class went into the hall we played Neighboring Numbers. We had numbers from 1–28.
RULES: the rules are someone calls out a number say 3 you would have to try and get TWO or three numbers to make 3. The numbers that I could not do were 1, 2, 4, 8, 16, 32, 34, 38 and 40. I was number 4. I think the pattern is you will never get an odd number next to an odd number. Or an even number next to an even number. I thought it was good it was a bit hard to get Neighboring numbers. They called my number out but could not make it up to four with neighbouring numbers. (Hayley)

This morning we all went down to the hall. When we got there Miss Davies and Mrs D'Arcy gave us all a card with a number on it (1–28) and what we had to do was choose a card. Say you picked number 29 you would have to use neighboring numbers (numbers that are next to each other) to make up 29. I used 14 + 15. The numbers I managed to solve are 3, 5, 6, 7, 11, 12, 13, 14, 15, 17, 18, 19, 20, 21, 23, 24, 25, 26, 27, 28, 29, 30, 31, 33, 35, 36, 37, 39, 40.
There is a way that you can get all the odd numbers but you can't get all the even numbers. I enjoyed investigating the numbers it was fun. You can use as many neighboring numbers to make a number as you wish but the ansew has to be egsactly that number. I went up to 40 but you can go as far as you like. Another way is that you can never add two odd or even numbers wich are to gether for egsample you could not make a sum like this: 14 + 16 + 17 + 18 because there are two even numbers together.
It is easyer to write the sums down on paper than just to call out the numbers. The numbers I could not solve were 1, 2, 4, 8, 10, 16, 32, 34, 38. Here is a picture of us in the hall. (Nora)

Energy!

Before we did energy in a science topic, I just thought it was to do with human beings, for example, I thought it was things like: Running, Eating, Moving Around, and quite simple things like those. But now I have realised that it is a lot more, to do with Electricity, Stored Energy and there are alot more! I have learnt that quite a few of the different sorts of energy comes as waves. Sound is one, Electricity is one two! But as I said there are quite a few more than those two. I have understood Energy now, because our class has looked at energy more carefully. It helped me to understand because we went through different kinds of energy and what it all did, and how it worked. (Karen)

I think the topic about energy was quite hard to understand sometimes. I use to think it was something you run out of when you have been running a lot. I much prefur doing energy than matter. I think it was interesting to find out where it came from and how it came. I did not know you can only change it, because I thought you can destroy anything. I think learning about energy is important because most things in the world are to do with energy. (Tracey)

Tracey and Karen are twelve years old; clearly their teacher would not have expected them in one unit of work—i.e. three to six weeks of science lessons, to have mastered the concept of energy! Neither girl uses scientific language in her log but in these brief looking-back entries we discover that Karen now realizes that energy is not solely a characteristic of human activities, that energy can be stored and that some forms of energy come in waves. Tracey is grappling with one of the most difficult concepts of all—that energy is never used up, but only changed from one form to another.

"What I Now Know..."

The next two pieces from David and Joanne were written at the end of a half term's unit of work on reproduction, in their first year at secondary school. They had started with flowers, worked their way through the dissection of a female rat and completed the unit by watching an excellent documentary film showing the birth of a human baby. In their final lesson—the one after the film, they were given about twenty minutes to "find out" what they now knew about reproduction. The teacher made it clear that she didn't expect them all to remember the same things, nor to understand everything. She invited them to write down any questions that occurred to them as well as their new knowledge.

My Knowledge of the Birth of a Baby   David

It all begins on the 14th day of the month when the female's egg is released from the ovary and caught by the frilly bits of the oviduct. It then travels down the oviduct. This is the time for sexual intercourse. The male places his penis in the lady's vagina causing sperms to be released. The sperms then swim up the vagina into the uterus. They then swim up the oviduct and meet the egg. The egg can only be fertilised by one sperm. The head of the sperm goes into the egg leaving the tail and neck outside the egg. The egg then travels down the oviduct into the uterus. It sticks to the uterus wall and then grows a waterbag around the egg to protect the egg. The egg starts to grow bigger being fed by a blood stream. It is called the placenta. It provides food and oxygen. The baby takes about nine months to grow properly in the uterus in the mother.

If the female is not sure if she is pregnant or not she should ask a doctor if he knows. He will then tell her to go to the maternity ward. The nurse there will test to see if the female is pregnant or not. If she is she will have to go to special classes for exercises and advice about bathing the baby, changing nappies e.t.c.

When the pregnancy is over and the female starts to get contractions she must be taken to hospital to be prepared for the birth. Babys can be born early or overdue. At this point I will put a question down. Why does it take so long to grow properly? And why do so few babys die being born? Why do babys have to [be] born by zezurian births? Why do the placentas have to be taken out?

The nurse will start to check the contractions and the heart beat and blood pressure in the baby.

What I Know!   Joanne

After an egg has been fertilized it travels up the Fallopian Tube and heads towards the uterus. When it reaches the uterus it sticks to the side and stays there until it is born. The baby grows and [on] the unblical cord which it feeds from and gets oxygen from. At first the baby starts off as small as a pin head. When it is ten weeks it is about 30–40 cm. At about this age his legs and arms begin to show. He has a tail which I think is its coxix [spine]. At the age of 5–6 months the babies tail has disappered and is almost ready to be born.

By now the woman carrying the baby has got very fat. This shows that the baby is growing. When the baby is just about to be born she gets 10–15 minute reactions which show the baby is on its way. Sometimes it is hard for the mother to breath so she has a hand thing which she can get oxygen from. Soon the nurse can feel the top of the babies head. When this has happened the mother has to take deep breaths and soon the baby will be born. After the head has come out the rest of the body slides out. A baby usually comes out head first. When the baby is born a lot of water runs out of its breathing systems so that it can breath properly. Then the unbliacal cord is clamped and cut. When the unbliacal cord is cut the baby is freed to the big wide world. The baby is proberly washed then put in a warm blanket and showed to the mother.

About five minutes later the placenta slides out. What I don't get is how the mother don't feel it coming out. And how the mothers stomach goes down after she has given birth to a baby. How does the water sack grow and die. Maybe one day when I have had a baby I will find out. There are many questions I would like to ask but some are very embrassing.

All the babies waste products come out through the mother. The reactions get shorter and quicker. When the mothers stomach has gone down she is left with stretch marks. Do the stretch marks ever go? How are twins born? How are twins made? Is it two eggs or a spilt [split] one? How does the milk in her breast made? Does her nipple get any bigger and does her breast? Does the same thing happen to other land animals?

Constructing the multi-faceted jigsaw

David and Joanne probably had at least twice as long (twenty minutes compared to ten) as Tracey and Karen to recollect, and in recollecting to begin a reconstruction of their new knowledge. This may be one reason why they produced longer entries. At the end of a topic I would always be inclined to allow plenty of time for a thorough memory search to be made. There is also of course more of a natural narrative to recalling how a baby is conceived, evolved and produced than there is to the nature of energy! Clearly David and Joanne are still very much in the process of making sense and fitting together these recently acquired facts but equally clearly they have been given the confidence to start their reconstructing from whatever surfaced in their own minds—they did not have to wait for the teacher to demand a response from them, to several of *her* pieces of information.

Writing to Explain

In these next examples, pupils are writing specifically to explain to their teacher *how* they went about doing something, consolidating their own understandings as they put forward their explanation. In this respect it is again importantly different from giving a "right" answer. Here pupils are using writing to reflect how they went about the task they had been given. They are not just writing about the *what*, they are also focusing their thinking on the *how*.

Investigating Digital Patterns

Here is an explanation from a fourteen-year-old about how she tackled the problem-solving that was involved in the maths investigation she had been given.

Claire's initial problem, called "222 and all that," was to "Write down all the three digit numbers you can make using the digits 1, 2 and 7 once only in each number, e.g. 217. Add all the numbers up. Divide your total by $1 + 2 + 7$."

Now do the same with lots of different sets of three digits. What do you notice? Can you explain what happens and why?

Next—follow your own ideas—or . . . what if!!! . . .

a. You use four digits? five? six?
b. Two of the digits are the same?
c. You are allowed to use any digit more than once?
d. You are working in a different base?

Here is Claire's explanation of what she did:

I firstly worked out what would happen if I did the problem with 3 digits. These are my findings. I used the numbers with the digits 127 first.

She writes down the six possible combinations of 127, which added up come to 2220—and which divided by $1 + 2 + 7 = 10$, comes to 222. She continues:

222 was the answer I got for all 3 digit numbers. I did the same for 4 and 5 digit numbers too.

I then thought I had found a pattern to work out the answer. I thought that as each number appeared twice in each column of the three digit number the answer was 222. 1 appears in each column twice. Each number appears two times. As there were 3 columns then I would write 222 because its a 3 digit number.

This pattern seemed to work for the 4 digit numbers as well. The answer here was 6666—4 columns, each number appeared in each column 6 times. So write 6 four times.

But I got to the 5 digits and it didn't seem to work for this one as the answer was 266664, and each number appeared in each column 24 times. I expected (looking at my pattern) that the answer would be 2424242424 as they appeared 24 times and there were 5 columns. But I forgot to carry the number!

Because 24 is a "tens and units" number and not just a "units" number as the 2 and the 6 then it wouldn't fit in one column, so the two would have to be carried. As each one was 24 then $24 + 2$ (for the carry) = 26. So when you had gone all through the columns you eventually came out with 266664. This seemed a very inaccurate way of doing it so I tried something else.

Meanwhile I found a way of finding out how many combinations there will be in each case. I did this by . . .

For 3 digits, 1x2x3 = 6 combinations
For 4 digits, 1x2x3x4 = 24 combinations
For 5 digits, 1x2x3x4x5 = 120 combinations

This was accurate.

I then went onto another problem of seeing what would happen if I used 2 digits the same in each number.

For the 3 digits: 3 combinations, 2 + 1 + 2 = 5, 555 divided by 5 = 111

I got the number 111 for every 3 digit number.

For the 4 digit numbers I got 3333.

When I tried to write the 5 digits that I could do, it got very hard, so I found an easier way of doing it.

The first thing I noticed was that I was able to tell how many different combinations there would be for each one. This was always half of the problem that I did first. eg. Problem 1, 3 digits = 6 combinations, 4 = 24, 5 = 120, 6 = 720, 7 = 5040. Problem 2 (2 digits the same in one number): 3 = 3 combinations, 4 = 12, 5 = 60 and so on. So you see the number of combinations is always half of the Problem 1.

Once I knew how many combinations there were, I could work out how many times each number would appear in each colum. I did this by dividing the number of combinations by the number of digits. But I had to remember to multiply the number I had used the same twice. eg. say there were 60 different combinations and 5 digits, 60 divided by 5 = 12. Each number would appear in each colum 12 times, except for the number I used twice which would appear 24 times!

So then now I knew this I could add up the whole column. Once I had what each column equalled I could work out what the whole sum came too. eg. Say the column added up to 132, then I would write: 132 (1 digit) 1320 (2) 13200 (3) 132000 (4) 1320000 (5) (It was a five digit number). Then when that was all added up it came to 1466652. All that I had to do then was divide that by the sum of all the digits and I had my answer.

Then I found out how to work out what the answer would be. For a 3 digit number in problem 1 the answer would be 222. My theory was that if you added another 2 onto that and timesed that by the number of digits that there were (3) then you would have your next answer. This worked every time but you had to remember to add that extra digit.

For a 5 digit number the answer was 133332. So I 5 x 1333332 = 6666660. I added the digit where the numbers are consecutive NOT AT THE END. But I couldn't think why you had to put the extra digit in.

But then I found the best way of all to find the answer. I didn't have to add any extra digit and it worked for both problems. Here are the results I got:

I found that if you eg. use 111 for 3 digits, 1111 for 4 digits, 11111 for 5 digits and so on—you use as many 1's as digits. Say that we are doing Problem 1, digits all different—starting with 4 digits, use 1111 x 6. You multiply by 6 because that is the previous answer for the number of combinations there were. 1111 x 6 = 6666. 6666 is the answer for 4 digits.

$$5 \text{ digits} = 11111 \times 24 \text{ (no of combinations for 4 digits)}$$
$$11111 \times 24 = 266664 = \text{answer for 5 digits}$$
$$6 \text{ digits} = 111111 \times 120 = 13333320$$

Another way of doing this is to . . .

for 3 digits— $\dfrac{10^3 - 1}{9} = \dfrac{999}{9} = 111$

for 4 digits— $\dfrac{10^4 - 1}{9} = \dfrac{9999}{9} = 1111$

Both these rules apply to both the problems that I did—numbers that are different or numbers with same 2 numbers in them.

As a mere English teacher I'm not sure that I understand *why* these patterns work nor am I sure that Claire understands why—but she does understand *what* she is doing and *how,* and explains it with growing confidence as she proceeds.

I have a hunch that some of us need to verbalize our understandings of a non-verbal system like maths if we are to pin down patterns of significance. Claire's writing seems to be helping her to do this.

How Well We Performed as Interviewers

The next two entries are from a "low ability" class of twelve-year-olds who had been collecting oral evidence from grandparents on memories of the Second World War. They had discussed interviewing techniques both before they talked to the old people and afterwards back in class. Then they wrote reflectively about the "how" in their logs, looking back on their own experiences.

Jill (who prints her entry in a strong hand)

I don't think I was a good intervewer becouse I had a list of questions some were the wrong kind of questions like nan was on about the bonds then I asked a question that was nothing to do with it but I got a good responce

Questions I could of asked

1. Why do you think your brother got sent home.
2. how much money did you earn with you job.
3. did any of your brothers or sisters have jobs.
4. what kind of jobs
5. did your parans have jobs
6. what kind of jobs
7. what was the main type of jobs

what were good question or bad

1. What is the first thing you remember about the 11 world war. I think this is a good question becouse it is open question and you can get a long answer.
2. how old were you. I don't think this is a good question becouse it is going to be a quick anser like *18 year old.*
3. were you evaquated. This is not a good question becouse it didn't carry on with what she was talking about.
4. if so were to
5. if not were did you live. These two questions carry on with question 3.

I think I sounded not interested on the tape but I was interested the person can tell wether you are interested becouse you start looking around the room on the tape my tone of voice made me not interested.

The teacher commented:

> I expect she could tell by the way you looked you were interested. Of course the tape can't show any of that.
>
> I am impressed by the way you have considered how well you performed as an interviewer. It was a good idea to consider individual questions to see how they measured up to the requirements. This deserves a merit!

Mark

What makes a good interviewer?

1. A good interviewer gets a good respons from the interviewee.
2. A good interviewer is polite.
3. A good interviewer askes good questions which are clear questions, and don't answer with a yes or a no.
4. A good interviewer Looks intrested and makes incoriging noises, i.e. WOW!
5. A good interviewer asks follow up questions

Was I a good interviewer?

I think that I was not very good, because I had a list of question that I read out—whatever she said and I had some questions that answered with a yes and a no. Sometimes I asked follow up question, but not as much as I should. One other thing that did not help was that my mum the interviewee was only four at the end of the war, so she could not remember much.

The most intresting part of the interview

The most intresting part of my interview was that when I asked her wher you bombed she said no just brought the seiling down, and that her Dad drove a amo train to plimouth.

How can I improve?

1. I shouldent ask questions like, where you bombed? because it answers with a yes or no. I should have asked something like where you bombed if so did any one diy. [Teacher suggests in margin: What did you feel like when the bombs fell?]
2. I did not look intrested. I just wanted it over and done with, so next time I had better look intrested.
3. I shouldent have read out a set of questions, and I did not ask follow up questions. i.e. How did the war afect you? To which she answered very little and I just whent on.
4. I cut her short every time she answered.

How I Came to Write My Poem

The final examples of think-writing from students looking back to explain and to reflect on how they tackled a particular activity or piece of work, come from a group of fourteen- and fifteen-year-olds who had been composing their own "creature" poems after reading and discussing Ted Hughes' poem "The Pike" with their teacher. I quote each writer's completed poem as well as their accounts of the writing journey.

David

Perch

It hangs silently still
Flicking its spined armor up and down
His eyes eagerly watch through the cans and the weed
It hasn't seen its enemy

Swift, flick, pike surrounds perch in one swoop
Perch not fighting, not even sweating from panic,
Pike, jerk fires open its barbed void.

Perch glides away from its beaten enemy
It's spines saved it,
They launched into pikes ambition, and killed it,
Pike had to release it or die from the pain.
Perch has vaporized from my eyes.

River still still
Not a rippling wave distorting the polished surface,
The reeds rustle and moorhen flies away,
Pike will have to stay hungry today
For perch has hidden in the water drowned amazon.

Drafting A Poem

No one I know deliberately fishes for perch as they are good for keeping down the pike in the river. The pacific perch in this poem was large in comparison to most others and the pike had its work cut out from the start. The moorhen flying away with the upmost noise is typical although it didn't happen at that time I saw it on my way home. Pike are always trying to eat any fish smaller than themselves and they never seem to learn about Perch. The poem is based on typical movements of both fish and the line "Not even sweating from panic" is just so people can relate to the coolness of the fish. In the original poem [Ted Hughes' poem] Eater was used instead of pike and Enemy. This was changed as the pike doesn't actually end up eating the perch as the name Eater would imply. I was brought to the attention of this by the constructive criticism of many people. The main structure and description in the poem is based on not one but many years of fishing and watching fish. Hangs is used at the beginning of the poem as from standing on the bank of a river you cannot tell how the perch is staying in its position. Water drowned Amazon is just used to explain how the fish must see the weed forest in the river. Also like a jungle the weed is "unmapped" and forever changing. Also weed can cover very large areas of a river and it is very dense.

Noel

Tawny Owl

Tawny owl, soft, loose plumage
makes silent flight,
Silent predator, sweeping
throughout the night.

Stubbed tail and rounded wings,
Huge eyes—darkened brown,
Contained in rounded setting—
Out of proportion to the body.

Sleeping by day,
eyes closed to the light,
Oblivious to the noise
of small birds fluttering around.

Feeding by night,
the hunted's useless plight
selected and swooped upon,
In claws held tight.

Creation of my Poem

Before I even started to write this poem I had to think of the animal I was going to write about. I decided against writing about my Dog (which is what I normally write about in poems) and decided to write about an owl. As I know very little about birds, I got a book about British Birds and looked through until I found a suitable owl. The owl I chose to write about was The Tawny Owl because in the book it had a good detailed description and picture. I read the paragraph that went with the picture and picked out descriptive words about the owl and used them as the basis to my poem. Some of the words and phrases I picked were: "soft loose plumage," "silent flight," "contained in rounded setting," "small birds fluttering around."

I then set to writing the poem using more descriptive words to link the words and phrases I had found together. Instead of using simple forms of some words I tried as much as I could to use better and sometimes more descriptive words than what I could of used, for example instead of using "unaware" in the third verse (third line) I chose to use "oblivious" as a more interesting and descriptive word. In the second draft I change the words "short" and "large" to "stubbed" and "huge" to make it more interesting.

Paul

Toby, My Basset Hound

Smooth and round bodied,
Folded and pocketed,
Large solid paws,
Short blunt claws.
Shiney polished coat,
Ship shape as a boat,
Quivers like a jelly,
Around his pink belly,
He's always the fool,
And howls to us all,
To get his food,
(His manners are crude).
Tell him "Toby sit!"
And wait for a bit,
As he will curl tight,
His head out of sight.
When he wakes up,
He jumps for a cup;
With tea, on the sill,
Which falls and spills.
Toby isn't so bad,
He just looks so sad,
His large wrinkled face,
Ages him out of place.

I knew what my subject would be right away. It was to be my new Basset Hound Toby, as Bassets are full of character. They are also very sensitive and like to be the centre of attraction.

To start my poem, I wanted to discribe my Hound. I needed to express his cute, yet strange appearance. Toby has very loose floppy skin draped over a strong, low built skeleton. To express this I used the words "Folded and Pocketed." The word "Pocketed" comes from what are known as his pockets found at the back of his hind legs. Toby's are somewhat large. The word "Folded" discribes perfectly the many folds of skin on his front paws and the back of his head. The line "Smooth and round bodied" discribes his short velvet like fur, and the way his domed head and his bottom are shaped.

In my first draft, I wrote "Snoors like a goat," but I withdrew this statement due to popular demand, as there is no proof that goats snoor. Instead I put down, "Ship shape as a boat," as ocean going liners are always cleaned and polished to the highest quality, as in the Q.E.2.

I went on to discribe his habits. One of which is knocking cups of tea out of people's hands. He does this to get people's attention. This can be quite amusing.

In my first draft I felt that I ended the poem too sharply, it needed rounding off. So I explained how his large wrinkles on his face makes him look old even when he is only 5 months.

I chose these three explanations about how these poems came to be written from a class collection of explanations each of which was full of interest.

If pupils' finished products *have* to be graded for examination purposes it makes so much sense to have an account of the writer's *intentions* alongside the composition that they have worked at. It is clear from these comments for instance, that each writer has discussed his original draft with others in the class before working on a revised version.

What is unique though about having these personal accounts, is that they reveal the thinking that informed the composing in a way that we could never have perceived merely from a reading of each poem, however careful that reading might be. Perhaps we would have credited David with an inside knowledge of fishing—and had the strong feeling that Paul did indeed possess a basset hound from his loving and beautifully precise description; but who would have guessed that Noel had composed his poem from the attractions that a textbook description of an owl offered. In some respects I find his account of how the poem came to be written the most fascinating of all!

I would also want to emphasize again that if we are to acknowledge more directly than in the past, that these young people are *not* professional writers, but youngsters *learning* how to shape meaning through the written word, such accounts of the decisions they made as their journey progressed are not only informative but essential. If we are to award a grade for their efforts in any meaningful way, we must take more fully into account *intentions* as well as outcomes.

8

Towards a Whole-School Capacity-Based Approach to Learning

The "meat" of this book comes in Chapter 5, 6 and 7 which describe writing strategies for primary and secondary pupils and offer for the reader's consideration a variety of pupil responses: "from start to finish" writing journeys and also reflective writing which sets out to make sense of other classroom-based activities. The medium which has received most attention throughout these chapters has been that of written language—thinking made visible on loose sheets of paper, in handmade books, on computers, in folders, journals, learning logs.

In this final chapter I want to re-focus more broadly on the implications of a capacity-based approach to education which could give both a theoretical and a practical coherence to the whole curriculum for all pupils across all phases of their school experience. When the Bullock Report was published in 1975, one of its major recommendations was that "Every school should have an organized policy for language across the curriculum." Those of us who were involved in in-service work with teachers in the years immediately following this report, saw many well-meaning programs of staff meetings set up to formulate such a policy, trickle away into little more than common agreements on how to indicate mechanical errors in student writing—or into lengthy discussions about how best to introduce pupils to the mysteries of technical vocabulary, especially in the sciences.

In the same way that the word "Language" tended to focus attention on words "out there," neatly blocked in paragraphs on the printed page—and consequently on the surface features rather than the meanings taking shape behind them, so the word "Writing" has tended to focus attention on the *form* taken by finished products: "the short story," "the essay," rather than on how the act of writing itself can help the writer to arrive at new perceptions and fresh understandings.

If however we switch our attention from the *manifestations* of meaning-making to the meaning-makers themselves, we find ourselves arriving at a more dynamic—and a more educational starting point. Dynamic in the sense that it is concerned with the mental processes activated within the brain, educational because it seeks to draw out and to develop those processes as fully as possible for every child and every young person.

Let me reiterate in a paragraph, the gist of the opening chapters of this book. Excepting the seriously brain-damaged, all humans retain, recollect, re-create, reconstruct and re-present their experiences *in some form or another*. As Frank Smith points out, they can do no other *because their brains work like that*. All of us achieve these modifications and transformations of immediate experience because we can also verbalize, visualize, think, feel and do—a constant intermeshing of helical capacities which makes learning of one kind or another not only possible but inevitable.

If we acknowledge these common human capacities as the birthright of every child, whatever the variations in culture or class, there is much that can be done, positively, to develop such potential—at worst, in spite of an unsympathetic system of schooling; at best, with the enthusiastic support of teachers, parents, prospective employers and funding bodies.

So, with our eyes firmly fixed on the children and young people from whom we are seeking to draw the fullest use of all the capacities with which they are endowed—let me offer the outline for a learning policy across the curriculum—and across age groups, which I believe would provide a coherent approach to education that teachers and pupils could explore together in partnership, with or without the requirements of a National Curriculum.

First, for a "brainpower basics" curriculum to work, we need to be able to demonstrate convincingly to our pupils *what they can already do* but often take so much for granted that they don't even notice, or shrug off as worthless: "I mean if *everyone* can do it, what is there to be proud of?" So much for the ethics of a competitive society!

As I have indicated throughout this book, it is of crucial importance to reveal to children from the minute they enter school to the moment they leave, how successful they can be, as verbalizers, visualizers, thinkers, feelers and doers! We can either bolster their confidence by finding ways to convince them that this is so—or we can equally effectively find ways of undermining their confidence to the point where they become unwilling or even incapable of utilizing their innate capacities within the walls of any classroom. I applaud the title of Ken Weber's book *Yes, They Can!*, written about those students for whom schools had operated in this negative fashion, until they encountered Ken who was determined to restore their confidence in their own learning powers.

It is the system within which we are currently constrained to operate which reduces so many young people to a state of aggressive or apathetic paralysis. It focuses on their " failure" to respond to extraneous demands; it focuses on an "out there" approach, which decides in advance what must be learned, instead of starting *from the inside* with the capacities that every student possesses. It is this system, when we choose to highlight failure and inadequacy, that creates a whole additional bunch of "special needs" for just those children who have quite enough to cope with in the first place!

An Examination of the Different Implications Which Lie Behind a Skill-Based and a Capacity-Based Approach to Learning

In Chapter 4, I touched on the problems that can arise when we share the same words in common, but find ourselves interpreting them differently. This is especially the case when the words themselves refer to abstract concepts such as "learning" or "writing." We need to be particularly careful therefore, when we put forward suggestions for a framework that offers a common *way of working* to teachers, to define as precisely as we can our understandings of the many different meanings which may be embedded in a single "key" word.

For several years now I have found myself becoming increasingly antipathetic to the widely spread use of the words "skill," "skill-based" and "learning skills" in documents and discussions which purport to address themselves to policies for improving classroom practice. As this is chiefly because the various understandings of the "skill" label are rarely "unpacked" (but more often extended into a proliferation of other undefined labels), I am going to make the attempt to do a little unpacking myself, which I hope will clarify my preference for an approach to learning which is capacity based.

The recently published *Oxford Companion to the Mind* devotes three closely printed columns to a useful exploration of "SKILL, HUMAN." The opening sentence reads: "In everyday parlance, 'skill' is used to denote expertise developed in the course of training and experience." So let me start from there, with the notion that we can refer to any learner as "skilled"*once they have acquired* expertise, whether that be a fast crawl or a fast manipulation of a keyboard. I have deliberately chosen as my first examples expertise which depends upon the acquisition of "motor skills"— i.e., the ability to perform actions smoothly without conscious thought.

If we ask *how* such skills are developed (because after all, the questions that require answers if they are to be of practical use to professional educators, are predominantly " how" questions), our own experience tells us that principally such expertise comes from PRACTICE—the more time a learner spends in the pool or at the keyboard, the more likely she is to become a skillful performer. As I pointed out however in Chapter 2, when I was considering the human capacity to do, enact, perform, the act of doing is never "mindless" ; improved performance relies also on the learner's capacity to think, to verbalize, to visualize and to feel. The football coach highlighting for his team their capacity to think in pictures and to think in words, understood that physical practice alone cannot produce highly "skilled" performers.

Once a learner has become expert in the performance of a motor skill however, whether that be driving a car or disco dancing, we can make the assumption that such expertise can operate smoothly, without conscious thought, and has become an acquisition on which the performer can rely, given regular practice, without deterioration.

If however further variables are involved such as playing for a team, then additional skills are required. The *Oxford Companion* defines "three functional parts" for "almost every skilled performance: perception of objects or events; choice of responses to them; and execution of phased or coordinated action giving expression to the choice made." The writer goes on to maintain that "the core of all these skills, especially at higher levels of expertise, lies in *processes* [my italics] of choice and decision."

I would want to add to that comment, that higher levels of expertise which reach beyond "automatic" motor performance, without exception involve meaning-shaping in one form or another. If "communication" is regarded as "a skill-based activity" for instance—and "communication skills" crops up as a label on policy documents and even school timetables with increasing frequency nowadays, the implication would appear to be that pupils can be taught or trained in "oracy skills" and "writing skills" so that somehow, once these skills have been acquired, their practitioners will be, without fail, expert talkers and expert writers. But talking and writing both involve thinking—and thinking involves the shaping of new meaning. As Murray and others have remarked, for a writer, however experienced and "skillful," the act of writing is never easy. No writer who takes writing seriously can ever go into automatic pilot; the challenge of generating fresh thinking which will draw the writer towards new perceptions may be exciting—and at times frustrating, but it can never be taken for granted as an acquired skill.

How we can help a learner *to become skilled*, perceptive, and capable of making her own choices and decisions is NOT the same issue or the same question as "How can we *teach skills?"*—in my view skills are unteachable because, rather like the Snark, there ain't no such THINGS! But expertise, in handling a variety of media and in becoming a confident capacity user, there certainly is.

As I hope this book has demonstrated, it is perfectly possible to devise strategies that will encourage pupils to reflect, to make connections, to interpret, to imagine and to speculate. It is equally possible to devise strategies that will develop a learner's capacities to visualize, to verbalize and to explore how it feels; in the process, her capacity to perform is also likely to improve.

This is why a learning policy which focuses on the dynamic powers of the brain, powers which we all possess and with which therefore, we are all personally familiar, offers more attractions for the combined efforts of a school's teaching staff than any number of skill-based check lists. A capacity-based approach to learning focuses on what the capacities are FOR—to make sense and to shape meaning. It seeks to involve the intricate dance of mental processes as they weave between the unconscious and the conscious mind, in a pupil-centered endeavor which never removes the ownership of the meaning that is being made from the individual maker.

A skill-based learning policy on the other hand, focuses on the so-called skills that are to be inculcated such as: oracy, graphicacy, computation, approximation, discrimination, manipulation . . . (to name but a few) without suggesting HOW the hapless learner is to acquire these proficiencies.

How then do we go about creating not so much a learning *policy* as a learning *ethos*—a ceaseless learning initiative in a school community, which will build confidence, increase motivation and sustain the development of every pupil's learning potential throughout the years of "compulsory" education?

We can begin, as the teachers who have contributed to this book began, by offering strategies that will enable pupils to recollect at least some of that "knowledge of the world" which has already been assimilated, waiting to be drawn from the memory cells *inside their own heads*. At every opportunity, we can encourage youngsters to make such acts of recollection; rediscovering what is already known provides an excellent foundation for setting out to find out more, through reflecting on whatever memories have emerged—and through investigating some of the questions that stock-taking what is known, produces about what isn't.

Brainstorming, clustering, drawing, free writing are all excellent strategies for activating the process of recollection. Exploring further whatever memories have thus been rendered visible, helps to clarify and extend the meanings they encapsulate. In the course of such exploratory activities it is important, constantly, to draw children's attention to the demonstrable fact that they can readily generate a flow of thoughts and feelings in a flow of words or images—and can just as readily transpose images into words (audible or visible) and words into images, both inside their heads and out.

I do not regard these strategies as applicable only to the act of writing— or to any one area of the curriculum. They are powerful and educative *learning* strategies which can be used by teachers of all age groups and all subjects. Similarly, the *media* chosen for recollecting, reconstructing, re-creating and re-presenting can be diverse and at their most effective can intermingle and support each other: spoken and written language, graphics, maths symbols, music, physical activities, three dimensional materials, computers. All these *modes* of expression can be brought into play in any meaning-making endeavor.

Similarly the *helical capacities* through which learning happens, are none of them the preserve of any age group or any curriculum area but indispensable to all. I have yet to meet a teacher who will deny—after a moment's reflection, that thinking or feeling or verbalizing or visualizing or doing—in one form or another, is irrelevant to the understanding of his or her subject specialism.

Similarly, the *stages* through which any meaning-making needs to pass: tentative exploration, a first "draft" of the new patterns that are forming, revision to clarify and give a sharper focus, representation to communicate what has been learned—are equally applicable to all subjects across the curriculum, whatever the modes of expression that have enabled the learner's journey to progress—verbal or nonverbal, visual or kinetic.

That is why I conclude this book with the suggestion that a capacity-based approach to education can offer a common framework for the joint endeavors of any staff in any school from the smallest village primary to the largest comprehensive. If all teachers in that school community adopted a positive "Yes, they can!" approach to their pupils, offered similar strategies—and shared, explicitly, with every class their belief in the human brainpower of every individual, I believe that the quality of education, "standards" if you like, would improve *immeasurably*—and no doubt measurably as well!

A capacity-based approach also provides an *integrative* framework, sharing a common way of going about learning which offers coherence rather than fragmentation. I despair when I see the curriculum being sliced like salami into a multiplicity of separate compartments, which consequently have to become increasingly thin! Why *add* "information technology" or "computer studies" or "media studies" or (heaven help us) "life skills," in their own discrete little boxes to the timetable? It's difficult enough suffering the subject compartmentalization with which we have long been familiar in secondary education, without compounding those difficulties by adding *ways of working,* in isolation, to the overcrowded set of pigeonholes that already exist!

A capacity-based approach is necessarily a multimedia approach which recognizes that learning in every curriculum area can benefit from a range of expressive modes, and that teachers can help pupils—and help each other to gain from the media choices that can be made. I have seen excellent "picture journeys" which have helped children to formulate concepts of addition and subtraction, and carefully constructed three-dimensional models which have increased the understanding of secondary science pupils. I have seen pupils projecting—and in the process formulating their understanding of a science experiment through puppet plays and PE students reflecting in learning logs on how to improve their performance.

Common strategies, based on a common pedagogy, using a multimedia approach to the twin goals of making sense and shaping meaning; building the confidence of young learners by focusing on what they *can* do and encouraging them to extend those capacities in the pursuit of further understanding; offering choice within a strategic framework; allowing for the unpredictable to emerge as learners make their journeys with teachers as companions along the way—these suggestions are a far cry from the current pressures for skill-training, prescribed check-lists and rank-ordered tests. But as Hamlet said to his mother, "Look here upon this picture—and on this . . . " I leave you, reader, to decide which picture is the fairer.

References

Barr, Mary, Pat D'Arcy & Mary K. Healy. *What's Going On? Language/ Learning Episodes in British and American Classrooms, Grades 4–13.* Boynton/Cook, 1982.

Berthoff, Ann E. *The Making of Meaning: Metaphors, Models, and Maxims for Writing Teachers.* Boynton/Cook, 1981.

————. *Forming/Thinking/Writing*, 2d Ed. Boynton/Cook, 1988.

Britton, James. *Language and Learning.* Penguin, 1970.

Britton, James, Tony Burgess, Nancy Martin, Alex McLeod, & Harold Rosen. *The Development of Writing Abilities (11–18).* Macmillan Education, 1975.

Bullock, Sir Alan. *A Language for Life.* H.M.S.O., 1975.

Buzan, Tony. *Use Your Head.* B.B.C., 1974.

D'Arcy, Pat. "Writing to Learn," in *The Journal Book.* Ed. Toby Fulwiler. Boynton/Cook, 1987.

Flesch, Rudolf. *Why Johnny Can't Read.* Harper, 1955.

Hudson, Liam. *Human Beings.* Paladin, 1977.

Hurst, P. H. & R. S. Peters. *The Logic of Evaluation.* Kegan Paul, 1970.

Jacobs, Gabriel. *When Children Think.* Teachers College Press, 1970.

Langer, Susanne. *Philosophy in a New Key.* Harvard University Press, 1963.

————. *Mind: An Essay on Human Feeling*, Vol. 1. Johns Hopkins University Press, 1970.

Lawrence, D. H. *The Rainbow.* Penguin, 1949.

Macrorie, Ken. *The I-Search Paper.* Boynton/Cook, 1988.

Moffett, James & Betty Jane Wagner. *Student-Centered Language Arts and Reading, K–13.* Houghton Mifflin, 1976.

Murray, Donald M. *Learning by Teaching.* Boynton/Cook, 1982.

————. *Write to Learn.* Holt, Rinehart & Winston, 1984.

Nicholls, Judith. "Winter," in *The Midnight Forest.* Faber & Faber, 1987.

Oxford Companion to the Mind. Oxford University Press, 1987.

Plath, Sylvia. "The Arrival of the Bee Box," in *Collected Poems of Sylvia Plath*. Harper & Row, 1963.

Postman, Neil & Charles Weingartner. *Teaching as a Subversive Activity*. Delacorte, 1969.

Purves, Alan & Victoria Rippere. *Elements of Writing about a Literary Work*. National Council of Teachers of English, 1968.

Rico, Gabriele Lusser. *Writing the Natural Way*. Tarcher, 1983.

Smith, Frank. *Writing and the Writer*. Heinemann, London; Holt, Rinehart & Winston, 1982.

Taylor, Mildred. *Roll of Thunder, Hear My Cry*. Dial, 1978.

Vygotsky, Lev. *Thought and Language*. M.I.T. Press, 1962.

Weber, Ken. *Yes, They Can!* Open University Press, 1968.

Wilkinson, Andrew. *The Quality of Writing*. Open University Press, 1986.